Opening to Grace

Swamini Krishnamrita Prana

Mata Amritanandamayi Center, San Ramon
California, United States

Opening to Grace
by Swamini Krishnamrita Prana

Published by:
Mata Amritanandamayi Center
P.O. Box 613, San Ramon, CA 94583
United States

First edition: June 2016

In Europe:
www.amma-europe.org

In USA:
amma.org

In India:
www.amritapuri.org
inform@amritapuri.org

Contents

Oh Goddess, who is my very life,
Teardrops of my love for You are ever flowing,
Sparkling as they fall,
from the rhythmic chords of life.
Eternally in love with You,
I shall weave a garland of stars...

My eyes are brimming with tears,
My voice is quavering.
The lotus of my heart is blossoming
without my knowing.
Melted by humility, my heart ecstatically
sips the ambrosial nectar
You compassionately shower upon us.

Though I am an insignificant child,
Who is not graced by the noblest of fortunes,
I feel an eternal celebration inside of my heart.
Beautiful one, my heart has merged
in the fullness of Your beauty.

Oh embodiment of Truth, Knowledge and Bliss,
Oh Goddess of Divine wisdom,
whom the intellect cannot apprehend,
You reside in the chintamani
(the divine wish-fulfilling gem).
Sanctified by your touch,
my life has become blessed...
Steeped in bliss.

Praneshwari – Malayalam bhajan

Introduction

"The winds of God's grace are always blowing. It is for us to raise our sails."

—*Sri Ramakrishna Paramahamsa*

Divine grace is the purest, most magnificent gift that can ever be attained in this life – the grace of the Guru.

Grace will take us to the spiritual goal of life: liberation from all suffering and true peace. We will never be able to achieve this goal by our efforts alone. No matter how hard we try in spiritual life, only the grace of a true Master can take us home.

Divine Grace is everywhere; we just have to be open enough to receive it. It does not matter what kind of spiritual practices we do; even if someone is far away, across the other side of the world, if their mind and thoughts are with Amma, they can earn Her grace.

There are people who may get lots of attention from Amma, which is always wonderful, but this will not necessarily give them lasting peace of mind. What matters most is that we earn the transforming power of grace from the Guru.

The essential question then becomes: how do we open ourselves up to receive Divine grace? It is when we open our heart and do good actions *every day* that the outpouring of God's grace begins to flow.

In theory it is so very simple:

Right Attitude + Right Action = Grace.

Amma says that selfless service is the most potent way we can earn grace. Selfless service and other spiritual practices create a purity of mind, which calms our thoughts so that we can become one-pointed and concentrated. A peaceful state of mind allows grace to flow to us and this grace will surely carry us to the goal.

Of course, you can live your life however you want. Just do good things whenever you can. Keep in mind that we cannot do anything about the *karma* (results of previous actions) that is due to come to us. We have to reap the results from all of the actions we have performed in the past.

Grace can certainly lighten this load, but ideally, that is not where we should focus our energy.

Instead, place your attention on whatever positive thoughts and actions you can manifest now. Then, when the dawning of spirituality arrives, you will have the opportunity to understand who you truly are. The Guru's grace will manifest and begin to melt the ego away.

A long-term *ashramite* (resident of a spiritual community) once told me the story of how she met Amma, some 15 years before. She was living in New York at the time, after graduating from one of the top art schools in the country. She had everything: her own apartment, a decent job, enough money, good food and entertainment, fashionable clothes and close friends. Even so, she sensed that something deeper was missing. She felt unfulfilled in her heart.

'What is the point of life?' She often wondered, until one day she broke down to God, sobbing in anguish and hysterically crying out, *"There has to be more to life than this!"*

The woman consulted a psychic, wondering if that might give her some answers. "I see you are about to go to a place with rolling hills," the psychic told her. "It is there that you will reunite with your Mother. She has been waiting for you to come. She loves you so much and is eager to embrace you and bring you home…"

The woman dismissed the words as nonsense. She was planning to move to California – her mother lived in Milwaukee! Besides, her mother was quite cold and rarely loving. There was simply no way her mother would be waiting for her or welcoming her with open arms.

Within the first week of arriving in California, this devotee travelled out to the San Ramon ashram. For those who have never been there, it really is a land of rolling hills…and there she met Mother.

As soon as she saw Amma, tears flooded her eyes, for she knew in her heart she had finally come home. She has lived with Amma ever since. For the last 15 years she has dedicated her life to selfless service. Even though she has very little, she feels more peaceful and content than ever before.

Being present in the environment around Amma truly does start to change us from limited, mediocre individuals. Just like a butterfly emerging from a cocoon, we slowly begin to grow into genuine human beings, more attuned to practicing the highest values inherent inside of us. We cannot get rid of the stubborn ego on our own; it is almost impossible. This is the reason why it is so important to have a living Master. Only a living Master can loosen the strong grip the ego has on us.

With the grace of a true Guru everything will happen spontaneously, when the time is right. All spiritual practices are meant to prepare us to reach the state of mental purity and ultimate peace where our own true nature can shine.

We can achieve very little by our own efforts – Divine grace is *everything!* So why not do good things while we can? Amma's life example has always been to wear Herself away doing good for the world. Hers is an example of the highest order, one that we can only slowly grow towards understanding.

The power of Amma's love is magnificent; She is like a big bus on the North Indian tour that can squeeze everyone in! She is a huge ocean-liner that can take everyone across the ocean of suffering. No one is turned away or left behind. She can take care of everyone. Her grace will surely make life complete.

It is all very simple. We always complicate everything so much…

The Guru's grace leads people to Liberation.

Chapter 1

Values for Life

"Your values become your destiny."

—*Mahatma Gandhi*

Amma's mother worshipped the Divine in everyone and everything. Her prayers started the moment she opened her eyes each morning. Upon awakening, she would reach down, touch the ground with her fingertips three times and humbly bow her head with closed palms pointed towards the sky. Only then would she reverently place her feet on the ground.

Amma's mother did this every single morning and so did many others who resided in their village. In the olden days the village community lived like this quite naturally, filling their days in so many subtle ways with offerings of reverence to a Higher Power. Their lives were full of compassion, acceptance and selflessness.

Today times have changed. How many people these days spend much of their day thinking of God, or even thinking of others? Most people live trapped inside themselves thinking only of, 'me, my family and mine.'

Hindu philosophy has a good explanation for the self-centredness we see all around us. It teaches us that time is cyclic, as opposed to linear, and is divided up into four cycles known as yugas:

Satya Yuga: the Golden Age when truthfulness prevails. *Treta Yuga:* the Silver Age when virtues start to decline. *Dwapara Yuga:* the Copper Age when the inherent righteousness in society falls even further. *Kali Yuga:* the Iron Age – the age of unrighteousness.

Gold is the most pure and refined metal, followed by silver, bronze and finally iron – from which the weapons of war are forged. The decreasing quality of the metals symbolizes the deterioration of good qualities in human beings, and in life itself, as the different time periods unfold. Even the life span, height, physical and mental strength of people dwindles down through the different time periods.

Some schools of thought believe the duration of the different yugas varies:

Satya Yuga: 1,728,000 years

Treta Yuga: 1,296,000 years

Dwapara Yuga: 864,000 years

Kali Yuga: 432,000 years

They believe we have only entered into the Kali Yuga by about 5,000 years. We have just started to slide into the 'age of darkness,' which began with the death of Lord Krishna around 3100 B.C.

Other schools of philosophy believe the entire yuga cycle lasts only 12,000 years. According to them, each yuga lasts 3,000 years, and it takes 12,000 years to descend through all four of them. At the end of the Kali Yuga the cycle ascends back up through all of the yugas and this circle continues on indefinitely. Those who accept this theory suggest that we are now near the end of the Kali Yuga, which will finish in 2025.

They maintain that mistakes made in the translations of sacred texts resulted in great miscalculations about the number of years in each yuga. Although the length of the yugas is definitely not agreed upon, all agree that the cycles slowly take humanity through ever evolving and devolving material and mental states.

Many of us so clearly see how the world and people have changed for the worse over the last few years. The goodness of the world is becoming more veiled.

Yet, there is one redeeming grace that always arises in the midst of our most difficult times and deepest darkness: we are forced to cry out to God. This is a major blessing that can come to us when external times are tough. With the grace of God, if we turn inside, we can escape the 'dark age' and find the 'golden age' within.

It has been said that only 10% of people in the Kali Yuga will be good, and even then, the bad people will want to pull the good down into a cesspool with them. We do not want to get stuck with that 90%. Let us try to hold onto the goodness inherent within us.

It is becoming extremely difficult for us to avoid the temptations surrounding us on all sides. It is very hard not to be pulled into darkness when everyone else seems to be behaving that way.

Even here at Amritapuri, I saw a teenage boy walking around wearing a t-shirt that read, 'When I'm good, I'm very good…but when I'm bad, I'm AWESOME!' Today it has become so cool to be bad!

One of the professors at Amrita University was saying that last year the university computer system contracted a virus, which effectively wiped out thousands of documents throughout the university. It infiltrated the campus via someone's computer stick and was transferred through the printer system. Anytime anyone put a document on his or her stick to print it, the printer infected the stick. Then, when the stick went back into its owner's computer, it affected their computer as well. The virus swiftly passed throughout the campus.

Computer hackers all around the world create virus software that invades universities, governments and banks in the attempt to crash them, just for fun. Nowadays people create destruction simply for their own amusement.

When we look at the news, we see how much violence there is everywhere. All over the world people are killing each other for even the smallest of reasons. Violence is increasing as a result of declining values in all sectors of society.

If we make ourselves stronger by strengthening our good qualities, then we will be able to resist the temptations of negative behaviour that are influencing us, in gross and subtle ways, all of the time. It is Amma's hope that selfless ideals will blossom inside of us. When they do, we will be able to act in ways that offer something good to our troubled world.

On several different occasions Amma has been asked by reporters, "If there is one thing you could change in today's world, what would it be?"

Her answer is always the same, "Values. We should try to restore the values in life. Values are the substratum of our society. Without values, everything will become very loose and only disharmony will rule."

When Amma meets with people, one of the subjects She repeatedly brings up is the importance of human values. She reminds us, "India is known for its richness of spiritual values. These should not die away from the face of this earth."

Many people do not get good values instilled into them at an early age, and we do not realise the importance of these values when we are young. There are so many cases of young people with undeveloped minds having children. If we do not teach our children how to live according to good values, then when they have families of their own, they will not know how to live a life of righteousness and will be unequipped to pass this awareness along into the future.

When people are growing up, if qualities such as selfless love, humility and forgiveness are not taught to them by their parents, then it will be almost impossible for them to live happily in this ever-changing world.

Recently while I was going for a walk, I came across a small boy who reached out his hands to me and demanded, "One iPod!" It would have been cute, if it had not been so startling. I am used to children asking for a pen, or even money, but an iPod? I certainly did not have one to give him. What is the world coming to?

I only got my first cell phone six months ago...

Desires are the root cause of unhappiness. When we blindly chase after them they only grow stronger, leading us into deeper and deeper dissatisfaction. Spiritual values, on the other hand, bring us towards ultimate fulfilment and inner peace. Unfortunately, the world gravitates so quickly towards desire and only reluctantly towards goodness.

Amma reminds us that living by a value system helps us to maintain harmony and balance with our surroundings. When a rocket is launched, once it escapes gravity, if it does not have a target it will go haywire. It will not know where to go. Similarly, without a value system to ground us, our mind will jump chaotically from one desire to the next, never settling peacefully.

Amma gives the example, "Suppose we build a fort with only bricks and some other materials. It is going to collapse and crumble one day without the integrating force that keeps things together: cement. Likewise, values are the integrating force that keeps people together, minds together. Values are the cement of society."

Without this 'cement,' society is left with ever-growing gaps; we are not teaching our children how to distinguish between what is right from what is wrong. Instead, we are teaching them it is okay to simply follow their desires, even if they be selfish, without caring about others or the consequences of their actions. Unfortunately, the world today is one in which good qualities are quickly disappearing.

A young woman recently told me that when she went to visit her nephew's house in America, she found drawers and closets full of discarded toys. She wondered how this was affecting his developing mind. Every time he wanted something new, he got it, only to quickly discard it.

It certainly was easier for his parents to simply fulfil his desires rather than to discipline him, but she was sad seeing the way his mind was being conditioned from such an early age. She wondered how he would ever develop acceptance, focus and discipline, with such an upbringing.

Amma says, "In today's world we see that people have houses with all sorts of physical comforts. They have beautiful buildings with air-conditioned rooms and fancy cars, but still we see that some wealthy people commit suicide in their air-conditioned rooms. It is something much more that gives peace and happiness."

Values bring balance and harmony to life. Amma tells us that holding onto good values provides equilibrium to the rhythm of life. She uses the example of a traffic light, saying, "In the same way that traffic lights on the road maintain safety and control, a value system is needed to save us from major chaos."

Only when we learn to reach out and help others in some way will we become truly happy. It can be as simple as offering a smile. Making this simple effort is how we open ourselves up to receiving grace.

One day when we were on an international flight to Mauritius, a *brahmachari* (celibate spiritual seeker) ended up sitting next to a mother and her baby. It was *ekadashi*, which is a traditional fasting day for many Indians, and this man had made a resolve that he would stick to his fast on this particular day.

The baby was lying in its cradle for a little while but soon started to cry. The woman picked up her baby, but whenever she tried to put it back down again, the baby started crying loudly. She had no choice but to continue holding the child.

After a while the flight attendants began to serve food to everyone, but there was no room for the mother's tray table with the baby lying on her lap. She would not have been able to eat had the brahmachari not offered to open up his tray table for the woman to place her food upon.

At first he watched as she struggled to open the food. She could not easily open anything or eat at all because she only had one free hand. He offered to open up the juice container for her. Then he took her knife and meekly asked, "Butter?"

She smiled as he buttered her bread for her. Then he really got into the swing of selfless service and cut up her food into bite-size pieces so she could easily eat it. It went on like this for a while and she was able to eat her meal.

One of the others in our group came over to me and mentioned how sweet it was, so I had a look for myself. After spying for a bit, I went back to my seat and confided to Amma that one of Her celibate brahmacharis now had a big family!

Amma got up and peeked around the curtain to watch him taking such good care of this young mother. The brahmachari was delighted that Amma had come to look at him. It was instant grace.

Often bramacharis would be like, "No, no women! We want nothing to do with the women!" But there is a time when we should be able to cross over the barrier of our likes and dislikes in order to help someone because it is the right thing to do. (And you never know, Amma might just be watching!)

Peace comes only from spiritual understanding, abiding by good values and, most importantly, from loving and serving others. When we live our life according to good values, then God's grace will flow to us like a never-ending river.

Chapter 2

A Light in the Darkness

"How wonderful it is that nobody need wait a single moment before beginning to improve the world."

—*Anne Frank*

Amma often mentions that when She was young, there was so much love between families and a deep closeness amongst people in general. Her face lights up with enthusiasm whenever She starts talking about the precious memories of Her childhood. It is so beautiful to see and hear Her at this time.

When Amma was a child, the value system was extraordinarily strong. The moral and ethical principles in the village and in Her family were well maintained, creating a happy foundation for childhood and for life.

Amma tells story after story about Her experiences as a child in order to remind us of the generous way people lived in previous times. If one house did not have any food, the family could quite easily go to their neighbour's house to be fed. Even if the neighbour did not have much, at least they would give some rice, chillies or salt. From these few ingredients they could make some simple chutney.

No matter how little they had, villagers always shared with each other. Nowadays, if a neighbour knocks on the door to ask for some food, we might call the police. People often do not even know who their neighbours are.

Today, we guard our houses and hide our things when guests come over. Someone once told me that in their country, if a family was eating and a guest arrived and knocked on the door, most people would deliberately not answer it. They would pretend to be out just so they did not have to share their food.

The values of hospitality, honesty, kindness and sharing have started to die away. Things have changed in today's world, but Amma is trying to inspire us to reincorporate these universal values back into our lives, which is why She repeatedly reminds us how important they are.

We should try to live our lives upholding truth and righteousness. Those who live their lives based on selflessness, faith and charity, enjoy greater peace and contentment than those who do not.

Amma's mother always set the best example of the ideals of hard work, proper attitude, care and service towards others, as well as devotion and awareness in every action. She instilled a sense of duty and integrity through all the values she passed on to her children. It is all of these powerful and influentially persuasive good qualities that so characterised Amma's mother.

Damayanti Amma taught her children that they should see a guest as God and serve others as they would serve the Divine. She had so much love and concern for everyone, even complete strangers. This traditional attitude was typical of village people in the olden days.

Damayanti Amma always set food aside in case visitors arrived unexpectedly. She cultivated many root vegetables in her garden, which could be quickly cooked and served with some chutney or chillies.

She especially liked to grow *chembu* and *chenna* (root vegetables like yams) because they could be picked and boiled in just over ten minutes and then served as a full meal to satisfy any guests who might arrive unexpectedly.

The children had to wait to be fed until they were sure no one was coming. Sometimes they would only have rice water with a little coconut in it because their mother was saving the rice just in case guests arrived.

Little did Amma's mother realise that she had a Divine incarnation right in her house, an incarnation she used to make go without food sometimes in order to feed guests, but that was okay. Amma could handle it. She was happy when the food went to the guests. Amma learned from Her mother, right from the very beginning, to serve others first.

When I went walking one day in the village next to *Amritapuri* (Amma's ashram in India) the *bramacharini* (female spiritual aspirant) I was with mentioned that the father of the house we were walking past was always very sweet to her. She would often offer to help carry his things if she saw him while she was out.

He confided to her one day that Amma used to do exactly the same thing for him when She was young. Amma went from house to house to collect food scraps for Her family's cows. When She visited, She always helped the families. If She saw anything that needed to be done She would do it without asking.

The village man mentioned that Amma never spoke much at all (probably because She was silently chanting Her mantra). She lived in Her own private world, a world nobody else could understand – but She always smiled so sweetly.

Amma's grandmother always kept a clay pot of buttermilk outside of her house for anybody passing by to drink if they were thirsty. Anyone was welcome to take from it. This buttermilk was not just for family members or neighbours, but was left out just in case there were thirsty travellers walking past.

Every few days the family replenished the pot, filling it with more buttermilk. Her mother followed this same tradition, as it had been passed down in Amma's family for generations. Amma's upbringing was like that; Her mother always inspired Her to give, no matter how little they had. They never had much, but were always happy to share.

Amma wants us to make an effort to discover and cultivate similar values, knowing that in today's difficult times, holding onto ethical principles is the only way we will be able to sail through all of the problems in life and be happy.

I love the story Amma tells about how in the olden days people used to have 'Welcome' signs on their door. Nowadays what do we have? More often than not it is something like: 'Beware of dog! It bites.' You will not find those clay pots anymore. People would probably steal them.

Amma said one day, "In the olden days there was a fear of not leading a *dharmic* (righteous) life. The thought of punishment for doing the wrong thing led one away from making the wrong choices. It was a useful fear; it helped to control the mind and kept people from making mistakes." Today there is not that kind of helpful fear. Instead there is only fear of a different sort, harmful fear, which comes from a lack of faith and surrender.

Even though it would seem that unconstrained freedom should grant us happiness, in reality, scientific research shows exactly the opposite. Research has found that those people who have a completely unrestricted check on their choices in life, in terms of sex or the use of drugs, end up being unhappier than others with more restricted lifestyles.

Many people feel that guilt is a completely negative emotion and is harmful for us, but I believe that a small amount of guilt can be quite useful in keeping us on the right track. People demand freedom, but in the name of freedom, they do whatever they want, often hurting others in the process.

A little bit of guilt and fear stops people from doing the wrong thing. Maintaining a small degree of fear in a power beyond our limited self helps us to be good to each other and to the Earth.

Amma wants to show the world the importance of good values and how they can be incorporated into our lives and used for service. All of us bear the responsibility to uphold these values – they are so precious and so rare.

We hear Amma talking about this important topic all the time in Her *satsangs* (spiritual discourses), but She does not simply talk about doing good things. She is a genuine, living example of all the best qualities in action. The depths of Her selflessness and compassion are truly unfathomable. There is so much we can learn from Her by simply observing the way She lives Her life.

Once while heading to the airport to fly from India to Europe, I noticed my shoes were starting to hurt me a bit. I put on some compression socks thinking this would keep the blisters from rubbing, but they were so tight they made the blisters rub even more.

As we were walking in the airport Amma said, "My feet hurt and these shoes are too loose."

I said, "Me too, Amma!" I was suffering the same thing.

Then later on She said, "My knee hurts." Just at that time, even though my knees had not hurt for years, pulling the heavy luggage caused my knee to start to give way.

I said, "Me too, Amma! Mine as well. It just started to hurt today." Every pain that Amma was experiencing, I seemed to be suffering from a bit too. Each time she mentioned some discomfort, I replied "Yes, I have that too Amma!"

Later on that day when we arrived in Spain, Amma had a terrible, splitting headache. Instead of resting, She declared, "I want to serve food to everyone who is here."

When I went to sleep later that night, I cried myself to sleep thinking, '*how ridiculous that I could say to Amma, "I'm suffering the same as You."*'

I felt so ashamed of myself. The little blisters on my feet or the little twinge in my knee is nothing compared to the magnitude of pain that Amma suffers. We can never really understand the depths of Amma's pain – pain that She bears for the sake of the world to help wear away our karma.

I am just so awed by Amma. Sometimes I cannot understand how I received the grace to be so close to Her, or to hear the words of wisdom that come from Her. It is simply thrilling to see the way Amma acts with people. No one could ever take Her as a normal human being when they get to experience Her fountain of unconditional love and deep wisdom.

Amma is giving Her life to teach us one central message. She keeps repeating it over and over again: do not let spiritual values die away from the face of the Earth. Spiritual values are such unassuming but precious jewels that we carry around with us wherever we go. If we lose these inherited jewels, only sorrow will replace them. Living life in a good way invites grace to flow into our lives. It leads us to the happiness we are always searching for.

Ethical values never grow old. In fact, it is the observance of *dharma* (right conduct) that draws Divine grace to us in more subtle and varied ways than we can even imagine. She is hoping that we will choose to change now, before it is too late.

Amma is trying Her hardest in each and every moment of Her life to set the perfect personal example for us. She is willing to undergo so much pain and suffering just to try to teach us good values and point us in the right direction. Let us hope that one day we can live our lives the way She does – thinking of other people first and going totally beyond our own needs and desires.

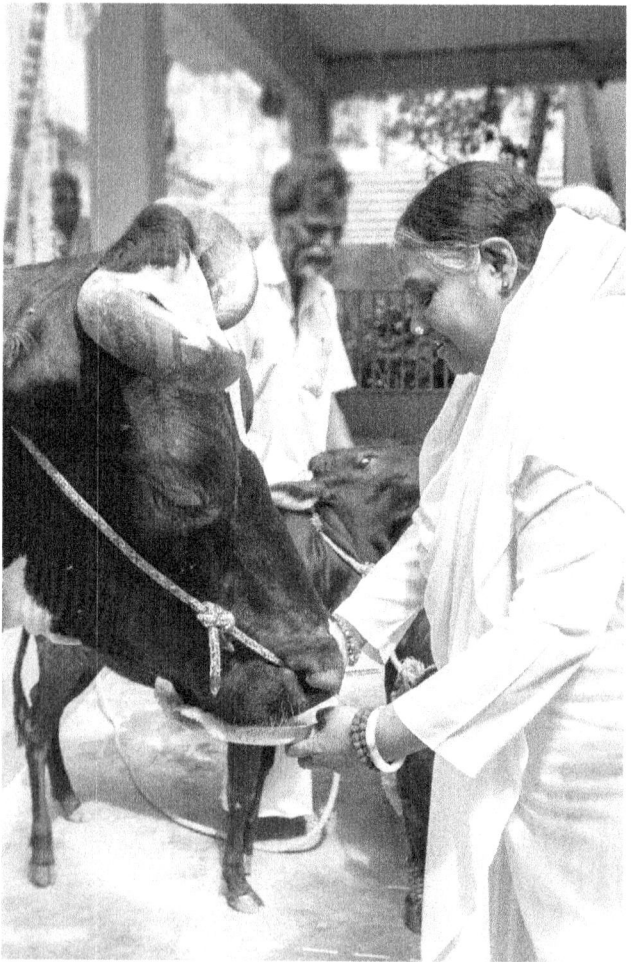

Chapter 3

The Sweetest of Cream

"Daddy, is Amma made of chocolate?"

—*Violet, age 3*

It is a very rare and precious chance to be able to share the company of a great, spiritually elevated soul like Amma. It is phenomenal to watch the way Amma moves through this world, bringing joy wherever She goes.

There are so many people who are suffering. Amma, in Her own luminous way, offers practical solutions and a cure for the pain of human existence, not just from a safe distance, but by boldly melting away all of our problems in Her soft and compassionate embrace.

It has been said that great saints move through the world with their consciousness up in heaven, but their feet firmly walking upon the ground. Amma moves amongst us, but it is truly as if She floats along in this world, unattached, like the sweetest of cream floating on the top of milk. Understanding the real nature of the world, She loves everyone.

A few years back when we were walking to our departure gate at the Chicago airport, a male devotee worked his way through the people so he could walk next to Amma. He looked a little sad, so Amma took hold of his hand. Another devotee was on the other side of Amma holding Her other hand. He whispered, "Amma, don't ever let go of my hand."

Amma was not shy to be holding hands with both of them as She made Her way through the crowded terminal. She is always the kind and compassionate mother looking after all of Her children – even though in this case they were both over 40 years of age. Pure love sees all as one.

Amma is able to see and feel the suffering of the world. But instead of turning away in sadness, She rises up to offer Her life in acts of service with a completely open heart. When we see Amma living in Her full power, we are inspired to develop our own as well.

Amma is teaching us through Her personal example, that reaching out to help others, even in the smallest of ways, is the greatest thing we can possibly do.

A devotee admitted to me that she had been anxious, depressed and selfish for years, and everyone kept on telling her to change. She resented them, even though she agreed with them and badly wanted to change. Yet, no matter how hard she tried, she simply could not.

Then she came to Amma and could finally relax because she found someone who loved her just the way she was, with all her flaws. This acceptance helped her to gradually improve. She said that she was so very broken and Amma loved her back to life.

Amma provides so many of us with a bridge of love to cross over a river of pain. In today's distressed and turbulent world, She *is* the answer to all of our problems.

Amma is inspiring people everywhere to try to live up to good ideals. She receives each and every person who comes to Her in the same special way: one moment advising the poorest fisherman in Her neighbouring village how to secure the next meal for his family; the next, conferring with one of the most developed scientific minds in the world about possible solutions for world hunger.

A woman from Los Angeles conveyed to me an extraordinary, heart-opening experience she had with Amma. Each time Amma visits L.A. this lady goes to be with Her. One year, she had seen Amma for two consecutive days and felt so full she decided not to go to the program on the last day. Her thought at the time was that she should give someone who had not seen Amma the chance to be with Her.

Friends called her during the day to ask if she wanted to come along with them to see Amma that evening. She told them all that she was not going. But around six pm, she began to feel the urgent need to see Amma. It was a feeling that would not leave her. She rushed and got dressed, knowing that the darshan lines would be very long.

She did not want to stop on the way, so she looked in the refrigerator to find something to give as an offering for Amma. She found a nice apple.

While sitting in the darshan line, she told the apple, "You are going to Amma. You are a gift for Amma to show Her my love for Her."

Turning the apple over as she prayed, she nearly had a heart attack when she noticed a rotten spot on the bottom.

She burst into tears, thinking to herself, 'I can't give Amma an apple with a rotten spot in it.' She was devastated but did not have anything else to give.

And so, when it was her turn, she handed Amma the apple.

Amma took the apple from her hand, turned it over and bit out the rotten part. The woman was stunned by Amma's action.

For days after her darshan, she was euphoric. She felt that Amma was saying to her, "I love you, no matter if you sometimes think you are not enough. You are loved unconditionally and I love all of you...even all the little spots that might not seem perfect."

Isn't that what we all long so much to know, that we are completely loved?

By this story, I do not mean to suggest that anyone should ever intentionally give Amma something rotten. The point is to convey the depths of Amma's love for us.

Life in the world ingrains in us the notion that we have to be a certain way in order to be accepted and loved: perfect, smart, beautiful, rich, thin and flawless – with no rotten spots. Nobody wants to believe this, but when we are bombarded with these messages throughout our lives, it has a lasting effect on us.

Amma's simple but significant act expressed more than words could ever convey. This woman felt so loved by Amma. She absolutely knew in that moment that Amma is the embodiment of pure, unconditional love.

Amma is waiting to share a taste of Divine love with us. We do not need to wait to become pure to approach Her. Her love absorbs all of the negativities from us and purifies us.

Amma tries so hard to take us beyond the false ideas that we have built up, feeling in so many different ways that we are *less* than worthy. She is able to bring us back in touch with our true nature, love. Amma strives to awaken the good qualities lying dormant within us.

Sometimes people want flawless gem-stones...but the problem is, they all have some tiny flaws. Mother Nature simply creates like that. Only fake glass has no flaws. We have to accept ourselves as we are and try to make the most of it.

Amma comes to us as a unique blessing, combining the wisdom of spirituality with compassion in action, while offering practical advice to help us face the problems in life.

She embodies the highest truth of *Vedanta* (one of the main systems of Indian philosophy) in all of Her actions. She sees the unity in life like a thread running through everyone and everything and softly tries to help us bring a change of vision into our lives – not by force, but by gently offering us an unselfish love that inspires us to grow from the inside out.

There is a little Hispanic boy who lives at the ashram and comes on tour with us. He is incredibly dedicated to *seva* (selfless service) – more so than most adults. Now he works full time for the sound system crew, which is a demanding, full-time job. He helps on the stage, assists in the sound booth and helps with the team's set-up and break down.

A few years back on Europe tour, while we were in Spain (before he was committed to a full-time seva team), he decided that he would put his translation skills to good use. He went around to every table in the bookstall and asked if they needed a translator. He carried a small pencil and pad of paper and created a schedule for himself.

Even if the sevites at the table knew Spanish, this little boy was too cute to turn down. Very soon he was booked solid for hours and hours of seva – from 10am until midnight without any breaks – one hour at each table. When asked if he was planning to eat, the boy replied, "Uh, well…I think my friends can bring me food!"

It was around 11pm when he was scheduled to work at my table. Of course, at the ripe old age of five and a half, and after a long day of work, it is needless to say that he spent his shift sleeping soundly in his bed (I also happen to know that he missed an earlier shift because his father forced him to eat).

The girls I work with playfully asked him, *"Where were you?"*

He was so cute and apologetic, saying, "I'm so sorry…I fell asleep…I didn't mean to! I'll be there today!"

Even if we may not have the most proficient, professional skills to be able to do really important things, just developing sincerity along with a compassionate heart and the desire to serve will enable us to tap into a higher energy.

A smile, or even the smallest good thought, can help initiate the underlying creative energy flowing through this world to come to us, empowering us to accomplish great things.

Once when a businessman was visiting a cold European country, a colleague offered to pick him up at his hotel every morning for work. The weather was brutally cold there; snow seemed to drift endlessly through the brisk air. On the first morning they arrived early at the company, long before anyone else, yet the colleague parked all the way in the back of the large parking lot, far away from the entrance to their workplace.

His colleague did the same day after day. On the first day the businessman did not say anything; he also managed to hold his tongue on the second and third days. But by the fourth morning he had to ask, "When there are no other cars in the parking lot, why do you always park so far away from the entrance?"

His colleague replied, "Since we arrive early, we have the time to walk, but whoever arrives late will surely want a place close to the door."

The businessman was extremely surprised to hear his colleague's reply. He had never known that it was even possible to have so much consideration for others. When our heart and mind remain open, we can learn something from every person we meet and every circumstance we encounter.

I remember one evening, at the start of a U.S. tour at the end of May, seeing a young girl who was being taken off to bed by her mother. She waved at me as she walked past and called out, *"Happy New Year!"*

It seemed funny at first and very cute. But then I realised how absolutely profound it really was. We should begin to think like this too.

Every day is a wonderful new beginning for us, filled with the opportunity to do something worthwhile or work on ourselves to change. It is never too late.

For more than 40 years Amma has held people close every day, pressing them against Her cheek to soothe away their pain. Some may feel that Miss Universe is the most attractive person in the world, with the prettiest, clearest, most perfect skin…but I think that Amma's skin is far more beautiful because of the bruises She bears, marking how She has given Her love away.

Amma's life is filled with beauty because She is wearing Herself away for the sake of the world. Hopefully, one day we too can become that lovely, by developing the capacity to offer something good to the world through all of our thoughts and actions.

Chapter 4

Waves of Compassion

"I could write
100 poems about
Her eyes,
100 more about
Her smile, and
That would not
Even match the
Shadow of Her
Beauty's radiance."
—*Brett Harbach*

Amma's life is an offering from the Divine, an offering to the spark of that same radiant spirit inherent in every soul. It really is remarkable how many lives have been transformed from unimaginable suffering to peace, simply through the power of pure love.

Some deeply touching examples come from the children who live at Amma's orphanage.

These stories illustrate so clearly the depths of Amma's compassion and grace.

Here is one such story:

I married my husband fairly recently. For both of us, life was a long, tragic story before we came to live with Amma, two stories soaked in tears.

I came from a small, beautiful village blessed with a river, hills and rubber plantations…our house was not much more than a thatched hut. Six of us lived there, including my younger sister and grandparents. My father worked for daily wages tapping rubber trees.

We were always half-starving. My father, being an alcoholic, used to beat my mother. Rare were the occasions when I saw her without tears in her eyes.

My father would always waste all the money he earned on alcohol and other non-essential things. My mother had to struggle just to make sure our daily needs were fulfilled, but the beatings she would get for this were unimaginable.

In all those years, I don't think we had even one moment of happiness. I used to often wonder why we were born.

I was not so bad in school so somehow I reached up to ninth standard. It was then that my father developed severe mental problems: he thought ghosts were haunting him. He fell slave to drugs and with that, our family headed towards destruction.

Every day my father sharpened a butcher's knife and kept it ready to kill my mother. Not one night did we sleep without fear. My sister and I shivered in fright if we ever even saw our father's shadow. Each day we would pray, "May night never come." Then at night, we would cuddle close to our mother.

We literally lived in the shadow of death.

One day, in the month of December, while writing my exams, I was asked to see the teacher as soon as I finished. When I went to the teacher, she said, "Daughter, you must go home. Your mother had an accident. Don't worry; it's not serious. She was cutting firewood and hit her foot with the axe, so you should go home at once."

For some reason, I didn't doubt her.

From a distance, I noticed a crowd gathered in front of my house. Seeing me approaching, some of my neighbours came and held me tight and took me away to a relative's house. I knew something serious had happened. When I enquired about my mother, they said she was in the hospital and that my father was with her.

In the meantime, I saw vehicles coming and going to my house. Each time a vehicle came I would look for my mother. Eventually a police jeep arrived. One or two policemen went inside the house. A few moments later, I saw them coming out holding a knife with a towel. It was the same knife my father used to sharpen every day. I knew then what had happened. My father was apprehended and taken to the police station.

My mother's dead body was brought home some time during the night, covered with a sheet. I drew back the sheet and saw my mother's face covered in stitches, totally unrecognisable. I don't know what happened after that. When I regained consciousness, people were sitting around fanning me.

I remember that I was woken by the sound of my sister crying. Then all emotions drained out of me and my mind went into a stone-like stillness. I became numb. Were there tears in my eyes? I don't know. Part of me was happy that my mother had escaped from the hell that was our family life.

After that, my sister and I never returned home again. We stayed with our uncle. The lives of all of our relatives were more or less the same as ours – drinking, beatings and starving. In the end, it was decided to send us to an orphanage. It was more than I could bear; I broke down sobbing. No one said a word.

The next day we reached Amritapuri.

I read somewhere that if God gives us a big sorrow today, it is actually meant to prepare us for happiness tomorrow. My life proved to me that this is true. I did not know then that from the hands of a beggar, I was going to fall into the lap of the Empress of love and compassion.

Amma was giving darshan when we arrived. I looked at Her with awe and wonder. For some reason, I couldn't take my eyes from Her face. Like dark clouds being dissipated by a cool wind, the darkness in my heart faded away.

Amma was told all about us. They showed Her the newspaper article about our mother's murder as well. The entire time Amma was listening to our story, She was looking at my sister and me. After hearing everything Amma nodded Her head, appearing to accept us.

Amma said She would enrol us in the orphanage and school in Parippally, and that She wanted us to study as much as possible. Then Amma embraced us both. She held us tightly and showered us with kisses. We had never experienced such love before, not even from our birth mother. The bliss and peace we experienced was beyond words.

Amma said, "Don't be sad, children. Amma is here for you. Amma will help you study as much as you want." For some reason when Amma said this, the conviction, 'This is your real Mother' entered me. All of my experiences thereafter have only made this conviction stronger.

We joined the Parippally School. Though hostel life was new to us, it really felt like one big, happy family. There were many different kinds of kids, including tribal children, studying and living there. Quite a number of children had come from conditions even worse than ours.

Since there was so much mutual affection, like in a real family, none of us felt that we had come from somewhere outside. Happy days passed quickly with playing, laughing and studying.

As the court case against our father progressed, we had to go to the court to give statements as witnesses. When I saw my father, hidden memories of my mother surfaced. In the grip of disgust and grief, I couldn't even look at his face.

When we visited the ashram, I told Amma about this incident. Holding me tightly to Her, Amma said, "What's there to bother, my child? Don't you have Amma now?" Such a buoyancy of love and motherly affection! How can I explain it? Once again all those haunting memories left me.

For the first time in our lives, we saw a cultural program while studying in the Parippally School. Amma had asked us to learn traditional art forms, including *Koodiyattam* (a traditional Sanskrit drama style of Kerala). We got many awards for these at district and even state-level competitions.

I was not poor in studies either. I got the highest marks amongst all the hostel students. When I received that prize, I showed Amma. She was happy and excited and told everyone around Her about me. Amma's grace was flowing to me.

In the early days I doubted whether I would be able to complete even 10th standard, but I went on to complete 12th standard as well. Thereafter, Amma asked me to get my BBM (Bachelor's of Business & Management) degree from Amrita University.

After I graduated, Amma recommended that I work for a few years and then go on to get my MBA. She then offered me a job at Amrita University. She said that, this way, I would have more experience and benefit more from my MBA once I got it.

During Amma's 60th birthday celebrations, Amma adopted 101 villages all over India for their sustainable development. New projects have been initiated as part of this initiative, and my job is serving in one of them.

Two months into the job, a woman who lives in Amritapuri asked me if I would marry her son. I replied, "If Amma agrees, I will also agree." I then told Amma about this.

She said, "You two meet and talk. If both of you are interested, I shall perform your wedding." I felt very happy because that family was also living under Amma's care.

My husband's background has been filled with pain, just like mine. This made us feel an immediate bond of compassion for each other and brought our hearts together.

One thing I am certain of: thanks to Amma's care and love, the family we will create together will be much happier than the ones we were raised in.

Amma's love has transformed innumerable lives. When we see the sacrifices She makes every day to serve everyone, it makes it easier for us to put forth some kind of effort. She truly is a living example of unconditional love.

Countless people love Amma's outer form so deeply – but to love Her completely, we should try to become like Her on the inside. All we can do is try, smile by smile, making an effort to mirror even the smallest ideal of Her life and teachings in any way that we can. Every little good intention helps. Surely we can create something truly beautiful as an offering for the world.

If people could let even just a fraction of Amma's love shine through them, then millions of images of Amma could be created and the world would be truly blessed.

Amma does so much for us, but She cannot force us to become selfless and compassionate and live a life of service to others. That is entirely our own choice. She offers us the most She can. It is up to us to choose what we want to do with it.

Chapter 5

A World of Kindness is Built

"Blessed are those who can Give without Remembering and Take without Forgetting."

—Unknown

Every day Amma sits for hours sharing people's laughter and tears, joy and sadness, merging into oneness with them. She is the ultimate example of empathy.

When people realise that Amma understands their feelings and emotions, it establishes a bond between them through which Amma's healing love can flow.

Amma finds endless ways to gently guide us back onto the path of goodness. Yet, She also has to shake us out of the negativity that we are often attracted to. She tells us, "Children, stop destroying! This is not your path. Yours is the path of love and compassion. Yours is the path of empathy, of feeling the pain and happiness of others as your very own."

Amma often reminds us that we should not bother to debate the question of whether God exists or not. Instead, we must try to remember that there are so many people suffering everywhere and it is our duty to help them in some way.

We should strive to feel happy for other people, instead of jealous and angry when someone gets more than we do. When someone is suffering, instead of secretly feeling glad (as so many of us often do), we ought to allow our heart to melt in compassion and do our best to comfort and console them.

This attitude of acceptance opens our heart and fills us with peace and love. If we sincerely tried to emulate Amma's ways, we would find that the essence of Her goodness, which we are so attracted to, actually resides inside each one of us. If we are always looking for Her only on the outside, we might get blissful glimpses of

Her outer form, but lasting happiness and peace of mind will never remain with us.

There is a devotee who has known Amma for many years. When he was young he took lots of psychedelic drugs and caused himself some brain damage. He was often homeless and lived on the streets, but for 25 years he has been coming to Amma's programs. Every year he turns up somewhere to see Her.

He has so much devotion for Amma, even though he forgets that he has to take a shower and forgets that he has to clean his teeth or wear clean clothes. Every year we remind him and every year he responds, "It's *so* difficult to get soap or shampoo or toothpaste!"

He can be argumentative at times, but it is hard to remain cross with him for long because he loves Amma so sincerely.

One year he came up to me and asked, "Can you forgive me for what I said last year?"

It was the first time I could remember him apologising, but I could not even recall what problems he had caused the year before or what he had said. I replied, "Of course. I can't even remember...it doesn't matter."

That day he went for darshan, and then two days later, during the final program in his city, he said he was going to go for darshan again.

"Have you taken a shower?" I asked him.

"Oh yeah," he replied. "I totally forgot…I am supposed to take a shower before hugging Amma."

I reminded him of Amma's instructions, "Amma told you several times. She directly told you that you have to wash and clean your teeth and wear fresh clothes when you go up to Her."

"Yeah, that's right," he replied, "I totally forgot." After a long pause, he sadly mumbled, "Well, I guess I shouldn't go then." He said that he hoped that he would be able to find a towel and some soap so that he could wash.

I volunteered to get the things for him so he could go for darshan. I told him, "Come back in 10 minutes and I'll find you something."

I went up to my room and went through my belongings, realising that I did not need all the things I had. I found a bag and put some extra soap and shampoo inside. The doctor had given me some pain gel, which I added as well. I had dried fruit someone had given me and a bar of chocolate, and then I saw the new socks I had been given. I knew they would be ideal for him. I came across some ear warmers that I had never used, and I grabbed some noodle packets from the kitchen…then I went to the staff room and sequestered a few more.

It was just like Christmas!

I peeked into the Swamis' room to see what else I could find for him, maybe some peanuts or something. I put it all together with the toiletries in a nice little kit bag, along with the food and the few odds and ends I had found.

When I came downstairs, I realised that I had forgotten a toothbrush. Another devotee asked me what I was doing, and then volunteered a toothbrush and some toothpaste. We put it all together in my favourite computer bag (which I was very attached to) but I knew he needed it so much more than I did.

We looked around but could not find him for a couple of hours. Eventually, towards the end of the evening, he turned up, and I happily gave him his bag of goodies. He was extremely grateful – and I was too. He said that all of the things would remind him of us.

Later on, I started to sadly contemplate on all those years when he was practically homeless and it had never occurred to me to give him all the extra things that I had.

We think of ourselves as 'spiritual,' but we travel around in a selfish little bubble, thinking only of what we need and what we can acquire. How many people exist in this world managing with so much less than they really need while we usually possess so much more?

I cried myself to sleep that night, regretfully thinking, 'Why didn't I ever consider giving more to him before?' I had actually given him soap and a few toiletries in the past, but it was only now, when he seemed much more humble and less argumentative, that I realised that I should share more with him because he really is my brother.

We move through this world rarely thinking of others and their needs. We just think of our own, even though we really do not have so many needs. Amma is trying to teach us to flow in the same way that She does, always thinking of others.

Even when Her body is falling apart, She still wipes away the tears of others and tries to melt away their pain, offering every drop of Her life's energy to comfort those who come to Her.

What will it take before we can also start to feel like that? When will we honestly start to become *genuine* human beings, in the highest sense of the word? When will we stop living selfishly with our thoughts, feelings and emotions all orbiting around ourselves and our own small world, but never really caring about people?

Amma is setting a beautiful example for the world. She never expects us to follow completely in Her footsteps, that would be impossible, but at least we could start to try a little...

There are so many people out in the world, unsung heroes, who understand this truth and are doing their utmost to help, even in the smallest of ways. Their random acts of kindness hold the potential to make a real difference in people's lives.

The world is full of possibilities. Like all things in life, we have a choice about the direction we want to go in. When we walk into a supermarket, we can choose the unhealthy, greasy, salty food that is loaded with all kinds of sweeteners, or we can choose the fresh, healthy food that will make our bodies and minds strong. It is up to us to make the decision about what to reach for.

The Internet is another example of the endless choices we have. When people go online, they can choose to surf all kinds of destructive sites. They can view pornography, look up how to make drugs or even research how to build a bomb. On the other hand, we can choose to do something good, like read the sweet, hopeful websites that people put up to inspire us. Below are some beautiful examples, true stories that were posted online to uplift us:

> It was my first day back to school after being hospitalised for chemo. I had lost all of my hair, and was embarrassed. When I walked in, *everyone was bald* – the popular kids, people I didn't know, my friends, the teachers. *Everyone.*

> Today I met a girl, 17 and homeless. She said she was hungry, so I told her to come get lunch with me. Seeing her

attempt to get 10 cents off an escalator gave me teary eyes. As we left, she noticed a cold homeless boy and without thinking she gave him half her meal.

I teach High School. During a fire alarm in winter, I noticed a scared special needs student crying and refusing to go outside because it was below freezing. Without a word, one of the students took off her warm winter jacket and wrapped it around him, comforting him and helping him outside.

My girlfriend and I were in the drive-thru of a restaurant when we saw a homeless man begging for food. As soon as we got our food she asked me to pull over and she gave the homeless man her meal. When I asked her why she did that she simply said, "I can go home and eat a sandwich, he can't."

A while ago my overweight daughter stopped going on her daily run for several weeks. When I asked her why she wasn't trying to lose weight lately, she said, "Sometimes I don't come first." Much later I found out she was consoling her friend who had been raped and trusted only her.

Today, I was at my local park. I saw a little girl about the age of five. She had a *terribly* burnt face, from a fire. No kid would even go near her. But one little boy went over to her, took her hand and said, "You're really pretty. Wanna go on the swings?" She smiled and they swung together.

My 15-year-old sister snuck out and stole my mom's car. She accepted the brutal punishment my mom gave her, but wouldn't tell anyone where she went. Today my sister's friend's mom called crying, thanking my sister for saving her daughter from suicide.

My dad died in a car accident. I was feeling really alone and upset when my four-year-old cousin walked up to me and gave me a hug. Without letting go of me she whispered in my ear, "I'll hold you forever."

It is a noble goal for us to try and strive towards becoming more selfless, giving importance to compassion and other good qualities, instead of our usual greed and self-centredness. We know this is the right thing to do...so why don't we do it? How wonderful and fulfilling it would be if we truly lived by these values.

We have the opportunity to live in Amma's ways, to be Her eyes and ears, Her hands in the world. As She reminds us again and again, if we learn to love and serve one another, we will transform this world into Heaven.

Chapter 6

Love Your Neighbour As Yourself

"He alone loves the creator perfectly who manifests a pure love for his neighbour."

—*Venerable Bede*

Amma expresses love not only for Her family, neighbours and devotees, but for people everywhere. Amma sees Her 'Self' in us – the Divine Self – and She loves everyone as truly as She loves Herself. For Amma, there is no separation.

When you forget about yourself, offering everything to the world, the world will look after you. When Amma comes out every day to give darshan, She forgets about Herself and is totally looked after by Divine energy. In this way She can comfort everyone and still be taken care of.

She tells us, "If we don't put compassion into our actions, then even the word *love* will only ever remain a word. You will never be able to experience the truth of that feeling if your heart does not melt for others in compassion." We should try to practice this teaching in our daily lives instead of thinking only of ourselves. Amma is constantly showering attention, love and compassion on us, while waiting patiently for us to wake up.

One of Amma's devotees is trying to do just that. She runs a tea shop out of her home in England and calls it, 'Amma's house.' She has lots of stories about the grace that flows when we follow Amma's teachings and welcome everyone with love, especially in challenging or unexpected situations.

Here are two particularly sweet examples:

We named our house 'Amma's House' in honour of Amma's grace and to bring a little of Amma to our small town. Even if no one knows who Amma is, Her name is displayed on our door to bless everyone.

My tea shop is very small. It seats about 15 people at full capacity without much room between the tables. The entrance hall and doorways are not generous in proportion, nor able to be altered.

So in accordance with Health and Safety recommendations, and knowing how difficult and disruptive it would be to accommodate wheelchairs or large strollers for babies, I set about writing a notice to let visitors know that there was 'restricted access' for wheelchairs and strollers.

I knew that this might limit those who were able to come into the tea shop, but I wanted it to be a wonderfully peaceful place for our guests…

I managed to write the notice, but before I could put it up, the front door flew open and a very determined lady came inside, pushing an elderly lady in a very large wheelchair.

I did not have the chance to politely let her know the new policy before she started asking other people to get up and move their chairs. She was aiming for the much-favoured bay window seating area. Amongst the scraping of chairs, I hastily thanked everyone for their kindness in moving for her and resolved to get the notice up as soon as possible.

After the ladies and the wheelchair had left, I went to my back office to get the notice. When I re-emerged, there were two young women seated in the vacated bay window, one at each table – with an extremely large stroller, plus baby, firmly planted between them. How they had managed to get the giant stroller through the other guests I had no idea, but there they were…and taking up two whole tables (potential seating for five) between them. There was nothing to be done except smile and serve them.

After the baby and stroller had gone and the tea shop once again returned to peace, I went back once more to get my notice. I returned quickly, however, as there was suddenly a lot of loud noise.

A thrilled family of six stood in the open doorway, beaming from ear to ear. There was just one couple in the tea shop at that time, enjoying what had been a quiet pot of tea. They were as surprised as I was.

The family rushed as one into the room, some moving tables together, some diving across to choose their chairs and others making a bee-line for cakes on display with great whoops of delight.

The teenage daughter has cerebral palsy, it was explained, so the family would need extra tables to keep the china out of range of sudden movements. I looked at their daughter as they tucked a napkin under her chin in anticipation of the chocolate cake. She screamed and called out loudly with delight, her whole body quivering with excitement. Here sat beautiful, pure joy. I smiled and gave up. I threw my notice in the bin.

As they left, the family thanked me for making their tea such a wonderful outing. They said they would tell everyone else back at the residential home to be sure to come.

I cleared up all the cake and spilt tea, put all the chairs and tables back to their proper positions and put the tablecloths in water to soak. Then I laughed out loud. My idea of how the tea shop should be was obviously not Amma's. It was clear that Amma wanted everyone to be able to come to our tea shop – no exceptions!

And so it is.

Tea shop story number two:

It had been a very busy Saturday with lots of customers. We had worked all day with no breaks and were very tired by closing time. I'd had a threatening migraine all day and was feeling unwell.

At last the shop was empty and we started to clean up the kitchen and switch the equipment off. My waitress called out that she had forgotten to turn the sign to 'closed' and lock the door, and asked if I could do it. I went back into the tea shop.

To my surprise there stood an elderly man in an old coat, leaning heavily on a walking stick. He asked me if we were closed and if he could have a pot of tea as he was a bit tired. By now it was getting dark and raining outside, and even though I had been looking forward to collapsing on the sofa, I invited him into the warm and helped him to a table.

We got everything out again and made up his tray of tea. It was clear he wished to sit quietly without conversation. As he was sipping his tea very slowly, I told my waitress she should go home, I would make sure the gentleman was okay.

I busied about tidying the cutlery and re-stocking the napkins. After a while he called me over to his table. The gentleman wanted the bill and also to know about the range of teas we served.

I really did not feel very well, but there is a duty, a responsibility, being in Amma's house – even if only She and I know it. We have to be ready to go the extra mile if needed, and it should be with love.

The old man and I spoke for some time. I described the nature of the teas and fetched some from the kitchen so he could sample the fragrance of the leaves. Eventually the elderly gentleman finished his tea and took his stick as if to leave.

I made ready to walk across the room with him, but was surprised when he asked to buy some tins of the most expensive, rare teas I had. I had not expected him to buy anything other than his one pot of tea.

A few tins of tea may not seem like a lot to most people, but if someone buys something in the shop other than their pot of tea or coffee, it makes a big difference to earning a living. It is a great blessing.

For this gentleman to buy more than one tin of tea was a very great gift. My time and care had been given unconditionally and I did not look for anything in return – but a little something wonderful came nevertheless.

The beauty of grace brings quiet tears of never ending wonder and gratitude to my eyes.

People are always searching for the secret to success in life. The formula for success anywhere is so simple: do the right thing at the right time, even if you do not feel like it. This formula applies for success in both worldly and spiritual life.

One young man always likes to get attention from Amma whenever he can. He asks for *moksha* (enlightenment or liberation) each time Amma walks past – as if it is a delicious pizza that can be ordered at the café. Without fail, he places his order for moksha every day.

In response, Amma asked him if he had a girlfriend. He said that he did have one once. Amma instantly answered that he would not get moksha with just one girlfriend – he had to have two!

Everyone laughed. Later on, I realised that Amma's comments were actually most profound. With just one girlfriend there would still be time to think of himself, but if he had two, he would be so busy with them that he would have to forget about himself and work so hard to please them.

Now this was really just a joke from Amma (so please, do *not* go out and get two girlfriends!) but within the joke there was a layer of truth. Forgetting ourselves in service of others really is the fastest path to merging in the Divine.

It is so important to simply be a nice, kind, decent person and help people without thinking of the consequences. It works everywhere. It is through cultivating and sincerely trying to *live* spiritual values that we can learn to love everyone as ourselves and help uplift each other and the world. Amma strongly feels that this is what is needed in today's restless society.

Chapter 7

The Greatest Austerity

"Patience is the remedy for every suffering."

—P. Syrus

Dealing with all the different types of personalities we are surrounded by can be extremely challenging at times. We often forget that the challenging people who test our patience the most are those who have the deepest wounds in their lives. These are the people who need more care and attention to heal.

Even though we may not feel so fond of them, they are in fact our most valuable friends because they show us where we need to work on ourselves.

Amma draws many of these people to Her, as there is nowhere else in the world where they will be loved and accepted unconditionally. People are quick to reject others, but Amma accepts everyone, showing us that unconditional love and patience exist hand-in-hand. One will lead to the other.

A young woman once told me how difficult her family is for her. After she moved to Amma's ashram in India to pursue a life of service, they gave her an incredibly hard time about her choice.

The family we are born into is karmically bound to us for a reason. I told this girl that she should not unduly worry if they tease or make fun of her. There is a subtle bond of love underlying the relationship between all family members, even if it can be difficult to feel at times.

Our families usually just want the best for us and are afraid of what they do not understand. It is for us to be patient with them and show, through our good actions, that we have made a heroic choice to lead a spiritual life.

I told this girl that it was up to her to prove to her family, by her good behaviour, that she was not trying to escape the world, but simply adding to the beauty of it by offering her time in selfless service.

There are many spiritual seekers who may not understand why they have to experience the conflicts they have with others in their family, or even just with the people living next door.

We forget that *everything* is destined to present itself to us for a very good reason. Because of this we should develop patience and compassion for others. Try to look at the background of all those you have difficulties with, as this helps us to understand why they have become the way they are.

After putting her grandchildren to bed, a grandmother changed into old slacks and a droopy blouse and proceeded to wash her hair. Hearing the children getting more and more rambunctious, her patience grew thin. Finally, she threw a towel around her head and stormed into their room, putting them back to bed with stern warnings. As she left the room, she heard the three-year-old say with a trembling voice, *"Who was that?"*

When we lose our patience, we lose touch with our true Self and become unrecognisable to others and ourselves.

Truly, the greatest and most humble of all will have unlimited amounts of patience and tolerance. Sometimes I think that Amma's patience with us is even greater than Her love. She waits so patiently for us to change, without forcing us to accept any spiritual truths or principles. She simply offers Her love and acceptance while putting forth endless examples of goodness, waiting for us to change ourselves and find the true happiness we are always searching for.

One day while we were traveling on a plane, Amma turned to me and said, "The greatest austerity that one can ever practice is to have patience."

I was quite surprised to hear this, as our mind does not usually think of cultivating patience as an austerity, but Amma has met with millions of people in all types of situations. She has encountered countless, unimaginable problems and genuinely understands the human psyche with all of its subtleties.

The practice of patience will make us happy, reduce our stress levels and help our performance in difficult situations. Amma knows the solution to everyone's problems is to exercise more patience, but it certainly is not easy. As She reminds us, we must learn patience – otherwise we will become a patient! 80% of illnesses today are stress related.

While we were traveling in Kerala, local devotees wanted to perform *pada puja* (bathing of the Guru's feet) upon Amma's arrival. At the end of the ceremony everyone was anxious to get hold of a little of the holy water. With all of their grabbing and jostling, the plate of water was overturned and no one got anything. They totally wasted all of the precious water.

In our impatient desire to always take, we lose the most important thing: peace of mind in the present moment…or in this case, pada puja water!

I have heard some wonderfully amusing stories about the lines of people waiting for refreshments or the unending queues for darshan tokens where people will come up with the most ingenious reasons for why they have to get whatever they need straight away, ahead of everyone else and in the shortest time possible.

Sometimes people have even borrowed their friend's children and babies in an effort to look like new parents who need to have early darshan tokens, as they do not want to wait for long.

A great test of our patience comes when we are hungry and standing in a food line. In such situations, we might forget everything about reasonable behaviour in our craving to obtain a cup of chai, food or anything we need as quickly as possible. We feel that we need everything *right now*. Why should we have to wait with all of these other people for so long?

Amma has said that it is a great test for our patience when we are hungry and sitting in front of a plate of food. Will we still take the time to pray first before eating?

Someone was telling me that in some of the bigger temples they have 'express' darshan lines where, if you pay some money, you can go in the fast-track line to have a vision of the Deity. This expedited process is especially designed for the busy person who has more important things to do than spend time waiting in line, even if it is in a temple.

When there are thousands of people waiting in line for darshan with Amma, someone will have to wait until the end of the program and go last. It is often those who have the patience to wait until the very end who receive the longest, sweetest darshan.

Motherhood, in all its forms, teaches us about the quality of patience. How patiently a mother bird will sit on her eggs through rainstorms, high winds or burning sunshine, waiting for them to hatch. Birds must have immense patience to wait for their chicks to hatch, for if the parents try to force the eggs open too early, there will only be disaster.

When a child is growing in the mother's womb she must have the utmost care, attention and patience to put up with many difficult months of discomfort in her ever-expanding body. She has to force herself to have patience and perseverance both while the baby forms and while it is painfully born.

Then after the birth, even more patience is needed to raise the child well with all the demands of parenthood.

Anything great we can achieve in life takes time to develop as well as tolerance and endurance to sustain.

Patience is an incredibly rare and precious quality that is rapidly disappearing in today's fast-paced world.

Amma reminds us in Her satsangs – even in Heaven there is a long queue. If you are not ready to stand and wait, you might get sent off to the other place instead!

Although, I think that in today's world of declining values, the queue for Heaven is probably shorter, and the line for the other place is much, much longer.

Amma often tells the story about two spiritual seekers who spent many years sitting under a sacred banyan tree in meditation. One day sage Narada, the messenger for the Gods[1], appeared before them. They both jumped up from their seats and ran to him. They begged, "Tell the Lord that we have been meditating for so many

---

[1] Some of you may believe that there is not supposed to be a capital letter in the word, 'Gods,' but I cannot bring myself not to put one. In today's world, with the value system quickly declining, I want to give all Gods a capital. Every Tom, Dick and Hari gets a capital letter. Why can't we give God one? In my books, anyway, the Gods will get one!

years under this sacred tree. Please ask the Lord when we will attain God realisation. We are so eager to see Him."

Narada left and consulted the Lord. Upon his return the first seeker jumped up and ran to him. He asked, "Any message from the Lord for me?"

Narada replied, "The Lord said that you should count the leaves of this sacred banyan. That is how many years it will take you to achieve the Ultimate."

The seeker looked up at the tree. Over-whelmed by the thousands of leaves, he declared, "This is hopeless. I have wasted so much time here meditating under this tree when I could have been enjoying the pleasures of the world instead." With that, he walked away from spir-ituality.

The second seeker came to Narada and asked the same question, "Any messages from the Lord for me?"

Narada again replied, "The Lord said that you should count the leaves of this sacred ban-yan. That is how many years it will take you to achieve the Ultimate." The second seeker imme-diately started dancing in bliss.

Narada asked, "Did you hear me correctly? There are thousands of leaves upon this tree! Why are you so happy?"

The seeker blissfully replied, "I am so grate-ful that one day my Lord will come to me and grant me His Divine vision!"

With that, the Lord appeared and the second seeker was immediately granted Liberation. The moral of the story, as Amma tells us, is…"Infinite patience will yield immediate results."

If one thinks, 'Overnight I am going to become the greatest yogi ever, let me force my limbs to stretch this way and that doing yogic exercises,' what may happen the next day? You might pull a muscle somewhere and start limp-ing after your very first yoga lesson – all because you wanted to become an expert so quickly and did not take the time and effort to begin slowly. Some things have to be done gradually.

I read a story once about a teacher who held a flower bud in his hand. He showed it to a young student and asked, "Can you force this flower to open?" The student enthusiastically took the flower and tried to pry open the petals. He attempted to force the flower to open up and bloom. The petals simply broke off, disintegrated and were spoiled.

The exercise was meant to teach the students the importance of patience in our lives. For a flower to bloom and spread its fragrance, it has to open naturally. In spiritual life we sometimes want to force things, but we should gain the wisdom of patience. Remember, everything is set to bloom at the correct time.

Chapter 8

Learning to Respond

"Forgiveness is the fragrance that the violet sheds on the heel that has crushed it."

—*Mark Twain*

It takes years and years of spiritual life to learn not to over-react, as we all too often do. But if we can do our spiritual practices with the right attitude, and use *mantra japa* (repeating sacred syllables) and other tools of mindfulness as methods to help us control the mind, then somehow over time, our negative reactions will begin to slow down.

When people are young they react to each and every little thing. When we look at the face of a baby, a myriad of different expressions will pass over the face of the child within the span of just a few minutes. It can be amusing to observe this. When we grow older, however, it is definitely not so cute when we constantly react to all of the emotions that pass through our minds.

Instead of always instantly *reacting* to our thoughts and emotions, we must begin to learn the art of *responding* instead.

When we react, our emotions play the leading role in guiding us, but emotions come and go like the wind. They are not to be trusted. When we make them the foundation for our judgments, we usually end up in a lot of trouble.

The foundation for *response* comes from a much wiser place. Response is based on common sense and wisdom, not simply on instinctive habits.

Reacting to everything is a natural reflex that comes from deep within our psyche. This impulse arises from the fight-or-flight instinct inherent in us that has been passed on through the ages. It takes a lot of discipline and mindful awareness, learned over time, to tone down our reactions into a wiser and more discriminative choice of *response* to situations.

By conscious practice we can slowly gain a little more self-control. We can become the master of situations, rather than a slave, resolving the challenges that arise with decisions tempered by a calm mind.

Most people do not know about the evolutionary cycle of life and the inevitable repercussions that arise from our attitudes and actions. This understanding gives us the capacity to accept the difficulties that arise in our lives. Everything we do comes back to us in one way or another.

When we react in anger towards others, we must remember that at some time in the future we will be on the receiving end of this anger, as it will return back to us like a boomerang. If we can forgive and respond gently to the mistakes of others, we will likewise experience forgiveness returning to us as a blessing later on.

One woman told me a story about her family. Her cousin was dating a man her aunt and uncle deeply disapproved of because he practiced a different religion than they did. Her uncle even went so far as to make a scene at his daughter's workplace, demanding in front of all present that she break up with her boyfriend.

As her cousin went deeper into the relationship with her boyfriend, the relationship with her parents grew more and more tense. In the end, she married the man. Her parents told her, "It would be better if you had died rather than inflict this upon our family."

She stopped speaking to them entirely.

Six years and two small children later, her mother and father are desperate to speak to their daughter again and to meet their grandchildren, but their daughter refuses. She will not forgive them. She believes that raising her children around her parents, who are filled with so much hate and anger, will be bad for them. Their family, which used to be large and close, has completely broken apart.

If we can try to channel compassion (or at least use a little discrimination) when we see what our anger, jealousy and hatred does to others, life will become so much sweeter. We will receive the blessings of our own mind, which is a very great thing.

The waves of the mind will always be there, churning around inside of us with judgments and ever-changing emotions, but remember that every time you over-react, you will regret it. It will come back to you, in one way or another.

As we realise that our reactions hurt the people we love, we begin to gradually change and become more accepting. With practice, if we try to remember not to judge or get angry, we will witness our intense reactions slowly beginning to subside and eventually fading away. But be patient, it is hard to completely overcome anger, as anger exists inside all of us to some degree or another.

If someone treats you badly, it is because they have suffered so much in their own life. Forgive them and strive to be kind.

I was looking at a photograph one day; it was an unusual story of a battle between a small snake and a big frog. The snake had caught onto the frog, but the frog had the snake in its mouth as well.

An award-winning photographer captured the image and sat there, waiting to see who would win the battle. For 12 long hours he watched. In the end, he gave up and went to bed. He never did find out who finally won the battle. The frog and snake were completely trapped in their silent fight, which might have gone on for days.

When we fight with someone, we can really get stuck if we are not ready to be the one to back out and back down. The ego can be so dreadfully stubborn. One solution for devotees is to imagine that the person we are in conflict with is Amma. You *really* do not want to argue with Her – believe me. I have tried it a few times and you can never win!

Forgiveness is an extraordinary tool that helps bring people's minds and hearts together. It creates harmony on every different level, from our health and peace of mind, right through all the different layers of loosening our karmic bonds.

Here is a powerful, true story from a woman in Europe illustrating this point:

> I have been coming to Amma's programs ever since the first time She came to Barcelona. This time was different. Two weeks before Amma came to town, my life collapsed.
>
> I was walking down the street, just like every morning, when several men

approached and asked me for the time. I said, "I don't know the time," and kept walking. At that moment the back door of their car opened, and a hand came out and put a cloth over my mouth.

They dragged me into the car and put up screens so nobody could see what was going on, so people would assume it was just a couple wanting to be together.

I lost consciousness. I don't know exactly what happened, but when I recovered I had a man on top of me, raping me. I tried to defend myself with my teeth and nails, and I kicked him repeatedly with my feet. Luckily it hurt him, so he made a space between himself and me. I took advantage of that gap, and I gave him an even stronger kick.

There were other men watching him rape me, and one of them then tried to grab me – but he was too slow. I jumped out of the car and I ran and escaped.

I ran and jumped over a really big ditch and found myself in open land, screaming for help. I fell into another ditch that had water in it for irrigating the field. I started to wash myself because I felt so dirty. I just couldn't be that dirty. I couldn't feel that dirty. I didn't want that.

I had never looked for anything like that to happen to me. I had never provoked that to happen to me. I don't know why it happened. My only consolation was that perhaps by it being me, I was saving someone else…

I came to see Amma a few weeks later. I dreamt that She wanted me to come. In my dream She hugged me and told me She was going to help me out of all the pain I had. I believed Her.

I made the trip alone. My daughters didn't want me to come because they saw I was in a really bad state. They thought I wasn't going to be able to handle the four-hour trip by myself. But I insisted.

When I arrived the very wonderful Amma people helped me. I had no token number, but they gave me a special early number to go for darshan. When I got to Amma I asked them to please tell Her what had happened to me.

Some people have the assumption that once you're 'Mother's child,' Mother will protect you and such a thing couldn't happen…yet it did.

But Amma changed it all!

When She looked at me, while they were explaining to Her what had happened, I felt Her compassion filtering into me. With total trust I came to Her, full of hopes and emotions. I was sure that She was calling me in my dreams, so I came to see Her. When She first hugged me, I already felt that this was a hug different from any other hug I had received before.

It's not like She gave me personally a different hug than before, that's not what I mean. But I felt the hug She gave me was different – from it, a miracle started to unfold.

When Amma hugged me She put Her hand on my heart. I was telling Her, "Mother, please take away this pain. You don't need to take away my wounds, but just the pain, please take it away."

Amma looked into my eyes, put Her hand on my heart, and without removing Her gaze, She pressed my chest three times with Her hand. On the second touch, I began to notice that Her hand felt like it was going inside my body.

On the third touch, it felt as though Her hand, Her power and Her energy were all the way inside my body and coming out of my back – freeing me from all the pain I was carrying.

After my darshan, I felt that Amma's hand remained in my body and mind. I know that She is helping me to forgive these people. As a matter of fact, I'm already doing it.

Before Amma's darshan, I wanted to die, thinking how can I go on living having the memory of this every day? But I didn't have the strength to kill myself, so I cut off all my hair (before it was long, to my shoulders) as a sign of protest for all the damage they had caused me and for all the pain I felt inside. After Amma's darshan I was able to sleep through the night again.

I brought all my pain to Mother… and She took it away.

I never blamed God. I did ask, 'Why me?' But my faith was still there; even if it was a bit lessened, I never lost it completely.

The difference now, after Amma's darshan, is that I feel a complete, total, spiritual peace. Mother took away the pain from my heart. Now I feel as though I am beginning to climb up the ladder to Heaven.

I can't believe I'm the 'chosen one' for this miracle. But the biggest miracle is that I have renewed my faith in God… and in men. I am happy again.

I feel proud to be a woman. All men are my brothers and all women are my sisters. Everything is my own, and I'm beginning to forgive. I think that's the biggest miracle of all.

Amma is here with me, always. I feel Her love inside my heart. I know that She will always be with me.

God has put Amma on the earth for people like me, so that She can work such big miracles. Thank you Amma, and thank you for all the people who follow you and want to help you. From now on, I also want to help.

Heaven and Hell are concepts in our own mind. We create our own Heaven and Hell by our actions and reactions. Forgiveness is one of the ways that we can create Heaven inside of ourselves. The beautiful thing is, if you really try your hardest to forgive someone else, you will get more blessings than anyone – even more than the person you are forgiving.

When we hold onto anger and hatred, the only person who really suffers is us. When we forgive, even though the circumstances may be painful and the process extraordinarily difficult, we will start to find a little piece of Heaven inside. Often we carry around our pain for years and years, if not lifetimes. It is up to us to decide to let it go.

No matter how difficult it might seem, we must remember that when we forgive, it is ultimately for our own benefit. We must gain strength from understanding who we truly are and why we are here. Only then can we slowly journey forward and learn to embrace everything in life.

Chapter 9

Always a Beginner

*"All streams flow to the ocean because
it is lower than they are. Humility
gives the ocean its power."*

—*Lao Tzu*

A girl was telling me that she used to work as
a 'harness chick' at a parachuting centre. Her
job was to put the harnesses on people who were
about to jump out of airplanes. I asked her if
people often got hurt where she worked.

She casually replied, "Oh yes, there are a
couple of deaths every year."

"Deaths?" I asked, horrified. "Why would
anyone risk their life to jump out of an airplane?"

"It's fun," she told me. "Besides, beginners
never die, they always jump in tandem, strapped
to the back of an expert. And the experts never

die. It's the people who think they are better than they are who often get hurt."

"The thing is, you have to pull the chute high enough in the air to give a soft landing, but the better you are, the lower you can pull it. It's more thrilling that way. The people who die pull the chute too low in the air. Then they can't control it. It isn't really dangerous, but in their arrogance, they make a fatal mistake."

Just like those parachutes, we have to open our life with humility, *now,* before it is too late – because the ego really can kill us!

As Amma says, "We can control things only to some extent. Beyond that, it is Divine grace that makes things happen. We need to put in effort with an attitude of surrender. Even when we win a competition, we need to bend our head and bow down to receive the medal. Humility is the key that opens the heart."

There was a world-famous European movie star who came to meet Amma in India. Usually wherever he goes people crowd around him, fawn over him, stare at him and ask him for his autograph. In Amritapuri, however, he had quite the opposite experience.

While waiting on the stage for his part to be filmed in a movie production that was taking place in Amritapuri, he stood up to try and see Amma. Inadvertently he blocked an elderly lady's view. Enraged, she took out her umbrella and started poking him in the back with it, telling him to sit down. She did not know who he was, and even if she had, she certainly would not have cared. All she wanted was for him to get out of the way so she could see Amma.

Around Amma even the biggest egos get worked on (sometimes in the hands of little old ladies with umbrellas!)

Do not forget: it is all the hard knocks, the difficult people, the suffering and the trials, which hammer away at our ego and chisel it down. We never know how the Divine is going to work on us.

Amma's humility is beyond compare. When we went to Kenya to do a program there, as we were traveling in the car to view a devotee's property, I could see the local people along the way pointing and saying something. Curious, I asked the driver what they were saying.

He translated, "Which one is She? The one in white or the one in orange?"

When I translated this to Amma, She so humbly said, "I'm the same colour as they are – so *you* smile and wave at them."

Amma made me pretend to be Her and smile and wave at all of the people out of the car window. It was just such an amazing example of Her humility. She did not mind me pretending to be Her simply because She thought it would make the people happier and more excited to see someone different than themselves.

Instead of puffing ourselves up, we should attempt to humble ourselves and try to spend our whole life learning from everything in creation. Look at Amma. She has already learned everything that She has to learn, but still She opens Herself up to keep on learning. Either we become humble gracefully, by choice, or life will force us to be humble by making us face painful or embarrassing situations.

When She is not giving darshan, Amma can often be found studying different aspects of how to run the schools, hospitals and management institutes She has built. Sometimes She stays up all night looking into the formalities associated with running these things. This is how She is able to guide every aspect of Her institutions so well.

She never thinks, 'I know enough of this creation; I don't have to learn anymore.' She is always open to learning in every situation.

By opening our mind and heart, we will come to understand that the whole of life with all of its ups and downs, trials and tribulations, is truly an endless educational journey. There is boundless wisdom waiting to be discovered. Every blade of grass, every snowflake and even our billions of fingerprints are entirely unique, and each of them has something to teach us.

There is a lesson to learn from everyone and everything. Even if we feel we have failed miserably in the past, we should try to learn from that experience. Take a spider for example: if you destroy its web it just goes on building it again, never giving up.

Nature and all of creation is willing to share its most profound secrets with us, but we must open not only our eyes, but also our mind and heart to see the lessons clearly. If we can humble the ego a little and open ourselves up to learn, then grace will be drawn to us, and the mysteries of the universe will unfold. Life will become a beautiful celebration.

Life is a constant fluctuation of trial and error, which means that we will definitely (and frequently) make mistakes along the way. Some people scour magazine articles searching for magical secrets about 'how-to-do-it right,' but to no avail. No one is perfect, and everyone is different. I read an article in which a man quoted his boss as saying, "Show me a person who's never made a mistake, and I'll show you a liar!"

The good news is: when you make mistakes, there will always be someone ready to point them out and correct you. At least be happy for that!

During the *bhajans* (devotional singing) one evening at the ashram, a little girl was sitting on the stage near Amma, being her usual mischievous self. Each time she would start playing or being disruptive, I would turn to her and quietly chastise her, telling her to stop being noisy. She did not know much English, but even so she would usually make a face, then stop and be quiet for a short while.

After some time she would start being naughty, so I would again turn around and be stern with her, trying to discipline her. At a certain point, when she was being particularly disruptive, I turned to her and said, "You are just too naughty!"

She leaned over to me and whispered, "I love you…"

I must admit I was a little shocked at this reply.

She leaned over once again and repeated a little louder, *"I love you!"* She had a cute smile on her face, and I became totally speechless.

When this small girl got up to go at the end of the program, as all the other kids were rushing off the stage, she turned to me one last time and with a big smile and a big voice, she said, ***"I love you!"*** Then she ran off.

Like this little girl, we should make an effort to develop humility and be glad when someone points out our mistakes. The people who can do this flow through life smoothly. They are always ready to say, "Thank you for pointing that out."

Those with true humility bring a sense of peace and contentment, even joy, wherever they go. They light up the lives of everyone they come into contact with.

Can we be humble if someone corrects our mistakes? What if someone blames us for something we did not do? It is a very hard thing to be humble then, but if you can overcome the automatic rising of the ego that says, "No, that's not right, that's not fair and it is *not* my fault," and stop blaming others, you will see the beautiful lessons that start to emerge. So swallow your ego and accept life's teachings.

Take responsibility for your actions. Whatever we do in life has repercussions that come along with it. We will have to learn from them, whether we like it or not. It can be difficult to accept our mistakes, but when we do, we are blessed with so many beautiful experiences.

Here is one such example:

> After my seva I packed my favourite apron in my bag. Later that day when I went to retrieve the apron, it was nowhere to be found. I was devastated. I knew it was 'only' an apron…but it was my *favourite* apron, and I absolutely needed it for my seva.

I spent the whole day in a desperate search, but to no avail.

While everybody else on my seva team was busy sweeping, mopping and cleaning, I spent the whole day pacing back and forth searching for the apron. Every time I took up a broom to sweep or a cloth to clean, I quickly put it back down again in the frantic pursuit.

A friend came up to me concerned about the look of desperation on my face, asking, "Are you okay?"

I replied, "No! I'm not okay. I can't find my favourite apron. I bet someone's wearing it…I know it's only a 20-cent apron, and I shouldn't be attached to material things, but I can't help it. Never mind. I'm okay. I can't talk about it anymore."

Eventually after a deep struggle, I surrendered to the loss and decided to buy a new one. On the walk to the shop I started to contemplate all of the bad deeds I had done that might warrant such a karmic punishment. I realised that several days before, I had been very rude to someone I should have been kind to.

One of the girls on my team had unknowingly borrowed that very same apron. When I saw this girl wearing my apron I coldly turned to her and said, "That's mine. Just make sure to give it back when you are done." The apron was returned that evening and there were no further incidents of notorious 'Apron theft.'

When I remembered back to this incident, I stopped in my tracks and prayed to Amma, "Amma, I'm sorry for that. I knew that girl was having a hard time, and I wasn't very nice. I'll try to be kinder, even when it's difficult. The next time I see her, I will apologise for my behaviour."

Low and behold, I turned around and there was my favourite apron, covered in dust and hanging gently over the cement ledge behind me.

Someone once came to ask me about her spiritual confusion. She believed that Amma wanted her to fail. She went on to say that when she fails, she finds it almost impossible to forgive herself.

I told her that Amma would never want anyone to fail. She is entirely on our side and so much wants us to win. She is giving Her life to guide us towards the winning post.

At the same time, there is also a deep value in recognising our own failures. If we always think we are the winner who has passed every test, then our ego will only grow and become stronger; we will never become humble, like a beginner.

We must remember…we are always beginners on this path. Only beginners know how much they really need to learn.

We stop learning when we feel that we have passed every test and already know everything. There is a lot of danger in assuming there is nothing left to learn. The ego just loves to say, "Close the book. I know everything!" When we think like this, the ego only grows stronger, and how will that benefit us?

God is the embodiment of compassion and forgiveness. When we fail, if we accept it with the correct attitude, we will realise that we have the opportunity to learn something beautiful from that failure. When we can do this, we open ourselves up to absorb more knowledge and experience. If we allow ourselves to learn, perhaps one day we may even become an expert who guides others in the future.

Think of someone like Madame Curie. She kept on experimenting and failing, experimenting and failing, but she never stopped her work or thought, 'Oh what the heck, I've failed. I'm never going to do this again.' She always kept on trying, giving her life to her work. In the end, she discovered radium, which has been so helpful to humanity.

It is the same with all great scientists; they never stop learning. Thomas Edison conducted thousands of failed experiments, but he never thought of them as failures. Instead of dwelling on the thousands of attempts it took to invent the light bulb, he is quoted as saying, "I have not failed. I've just found 10,000 ways that won't work."

Do not think of yourself as a failure. This will drain your energy and can send you into depression, which can be difficult to recover from. You are an innocent child of the Divine Mother. When you do not pass some test, just pick yourself up, learn from your mistakes and move on.

If a toddler tries to walk, falls down and thinks, 'Uh oh, I failed. I'm not going to try that again.' How would it be?

Let failure make us humble. Use it as a positive growing experience to take us forward in life, as a friend that helps us to discover all the exquisite mysteries waiting for us. Do not focus on the negative side of things. Use everything as a positive challenge to help you grow. Then you will surely be able to experience the beauty inherent in all of creation.

It is Amma's prayer that each of us be able to find our path to success. She reminds us that creation is beautiful and just waiting to be discovered. With the right attitude, we will be able to see the world as Amma sees it. Have no doubt and never give up. Ultimately, you will win.

Everyone will reach the goal…it is destined.

Chapter 10

The Ultimate Tool

"Earth's crammed with heaven…
But only he who sees, takes off his shoes."

—*Elizabeth Barrett Browning*

Ideally, all spiritual practices are designed to tame the senses so that we can bring awareness to the mind and dwell entirely in the present moment.

With pure, one-pointed concentration, our refined quality of awareness will help us pierce through the veils of *maya* (illusion) that keep us under her control. When the mind becomes pure in this way, we will discover the essence of who we really are, and we will know who everyone else is as well.

There is a story that illustrates the importance of awareness for spiritual seekers:

A precious necklace could be seen lying at the bottom of a lake. Many people dove into the water looking for it, but no one was able to find it. Yet it was clearly visible for all to see. Finally a *Mahatma* (great soul) walked by and said, "It must be somewhere else. What we see is the reflection of it. It must be in the tree."

A bird had been attracted by the sparkle of it, picked it up and left it hanging on a branch of the tree.

Everyone was searching in entirely the wrong place for it. Like this, Amma is trying to show us that the real source of happiness lies waiting for us somewhere other than where we are looking for it.

We imagine that practicing good qualities is for others, or perhaps we tell ourselves that we will start to practice great qualities in the future, after we have finished having a bit more fun. The mind always tries to trick us, keeping us locked into our bad habits. We forget that we should start to incorporate honourable qualities right here and now, in our everyday actions.

It may take years of mindful practice before we can completely imbibe the essence of any great quality – especially as a first response when we are faced with difficult situations. We cannot afford to wait before beginning. If we wait too long, we may become too old to develop the habit of conscious awareness.

One day in the car on a North Kerala tour, Amma told us that one of Her devotees had named his three children Amrit, Ananda and Mayi. She laughed delightedly as She informed us. What a great way to try and gain awareness! Sometimes we have to strive to train the mind in an ingenious way before it tricks us into negativity.

Awareness is needed not only in spirituality but also for any interaction in the world to go successfully.

Everyone longs to get the chance to go with Amma in the car, but they do not realise how intense of a spiritual experience it will be. Once while we were driving to Chicago on the U.S. summer tour, we approached a toll stop, and the driver of the car suddenly realised he had not brought his wallet with him. He had no money at all. He asked Swamiji for a loan, but Swamiji was penniless, as was I.

Our driver had to jump out of the car and run over to another vehicle to ask for the money to pay the toll. He was totally embarrassed (but relieved, at least, that Amma had been sitting with Her eyes closed in meditation and had not seen his predicament).

One should always have *shraddha* (awareness) – and the driver of any car should take care to have some extra money with them for tolls.

There are times when I have told the people doing the security around Amma that they should be conscious to look after *all* of the people who are around us, not just Amma. They faithfully concentrate on Amma, but Amma's focus is always on everyone else. People can fall down in the throbbing crowds and be injured if we are not careful.

We have to have a conscious vision of 180-degree awareness around us and not just limit ourselves to the 45-degree angle of perception that most people live in. We should learn to expand our awareness to include others and stop cutting out the world like we so often do. So many people think only of their own personal duties and nothing beyond that.

Devotees often focus only on Amma, which is good, but we should not neglect everyone else. Amma is always thinking about the best interests of everyone in all different areas – in more ways than we can even imagine. Her awareness and care for everyone's needs is complete and all-pervasive.

If we want to progress, we have to broaden the realm of our awareness beyond our little self-centred world and care about others.

A devotee who works in Afghanistan, related a story to me that dramatically illustrates this point:

> Afghanistan is a dangerous, war-torn country. I've been evacuated three times in the years that I have worked there. I know the only reason I am still alive is because of Amma's grace.
>
> So many times I was very, very close to dying but at the last minute I was saved by grace. I will give you an example.
>
> It was April 5, 2014. Election Day. It was our job to monitor all the polling stations.

When I woke up that morning, I was not feeling comfortable about visiting any of the polling stations. I gave myself permission to follow my intuition. I knew there was danger, and I did not want to be in the middle of a blast.

I told a colleague that I didn't want to go, and he agreed, saying, "I think it's better if we just don't go."

As the rest of the team was leaving the hotel, they all inquired as to why we didn't want to go. I felt a bit pressured by my peers and so told my colleague, "Let's give it a try. Maybe we can go to the polling station at the corner of our hotel and see. If there is anything suspicious, we can always run away back to the hotel."

It was so amazing to see the lines of women who had showed up to cast their votes. About 350 women were gathered outside, huddled together in the rain, quietly waiting for the polling station to open so they could vote for their new president.

I whispered to my colleague, "Wow, this is amazing. Even in my own country, we would never see this." I was so impressed by the will of these women and their commitment to their country.

My colleague went to the male polling station and I went to the female polling station. They were preparing to open. There was one woman taking care of the ballot paper, another the ballot boxes, and a third, the polling booths. I turned my head and was so scared by what I saw next that I immediately turned and ran.

This was a female polling station. Only women were allowed to go inside; even my bodyguard was waiting outside because he is a man.

What I saw was someone dressed as a woman. 'She' was my size, and I'm very tall – much taller than the Afghani women. The person wore a black scarf, had very broad shoulders and hairy, masculine ankles were sticking out, quite obviously, from 'her' dress.

I called out to Amma internally, 'What is this?'

I heard a clear reply, 'Be careful. It's a suicide bomber.'

I was so scared that he was going to blow us up, but I understood that he was waiting until the 350 women were all inside. I absolutely knew that something would happen – after all, I was trained for this. I knew that I would be in the middle of the blast. My life had hung in the balance far too many times, and now it was clear that my number was up.

I started to run.

As I was running, I kept hearing Amma's voice clearly in my head saying, 'Go back! Go back and smile at him!'

I couldn't believe that voice. I would not turn back. That was suicide. The voice only grew louder as I got further and further away, 'Go back, go back and smile at him! Go back and smile!'

The voice was so strong and so unusual that I thought, 'Okay, okay. I know this voice is coming from You, Amma.

I will go back. I will try to follow Your guidance.'

I arrived back at the polling place, super-scared, like a small girl. The bomber wasn't doing anything yet, just waiting quietly for the room to fill. I walked up to him three times, but each time I got close, I ran away again.

I was such a mess. At some point he turned his head and I looked deeply into his eyes. He looked completely disconnected from the world. It was obvious that he was high on some sort of drug. He only had his mission: kill people.

When I saw his eyes, I wanted to run away again, but instead I forced myself to hold his gaze and to smile…he finally smiled back. Then he turned around and just walked out.

I realised on that day that I became what I always wanted to be: an instrument of the Divine. Amma used me to save the lives of hundreds of women.

Amma really is a genuine spiritual Master. How do I know? Because of the way She takes care of us all. Because of the way she always provides, the way She brings magic into the world, the way She heals and the way She guides.

I know Amma is my Guru because of the way She inspires me every day and the way She gives love to us all.

Amma often reminds us, that awareness is one of the most important qualities in spirituality. It takes effort, coupled with awareness, to invite grace. You cannot force people to accept this truth; you can only offer wisdom, helping them to understand the intricacies of life.

Awareness of the internal Divine Self is very subtle and difficult to develop. Therefore, we must start by developing awareness of the external, and this will slowly lead us to internal awareness.

One girl was telling me that during the course of her studies, she learned about a native culture that acquired its food from ice fishing. Every day the men would go out and carve small holes in the ice that covered the waters near their village. There they would stand, totally still and silent, holding long spears over the holes. As soon as they saw a fish or a seal, they would strike.

Even a momentary lapse in awareness meant that they might not be able to catch food for the day. In order to be successful, the fishermen had to develop keen awareness and total silence within.

The art of awareness is very subtle, and if we desire to achieve the Supreme awareness, awareness of the Divine Self, then we must start by developing external awareness in all of our thoughts, words and actions.

We have to be constantly alert to try and redirect the wandering mind. We need to head it towards something positive before it spontaneously dives into the worst it can conjure up.

Awareness is the ultimate tool to help us recognise and remember the truth: *we are not what the mind tells us we are.*

Chapter 11

From Love to Seva

*"Sometimes I just look up,
smile and say,
'I know that was You, God!
Thanks!'"*

—*Unknown*

There is a traditional story about Lord Vishnu and his disciple Narada. Narada wanted to see Lord Vishnu's greatest devotee. Vishnu pointed out the window and said, "It's that farmer out there." Narada looked out in surprise at the farmer. He decided to watch him for a day.

When the farmer awoke at the beginning of each day, he said Lord Vishnu's name once. Then he worked hard all day, came back at night and repeated the Divine name once more before going to bed. How on earth was Vishnu declaring that this was his greatest disciple?

The innocent attitude of a one-pointed, dedicated prayer to God, even in just a couple of words, goes straight to the source. Furthermore, acting responsibly and sincerely *is* the vehicle to express our devotion. It does not take very much at all to melt the heart of God.

People want to run after Amma (often by pushing others out of the way), stare at Her and touch Her as She walks past, but that alone will not help us grow in life. Crazy devotion tends to make us more hysterical, but after the rush of emotion, we may still remain rooted in selfishness.

It is a sad truth that some so-called 'devotional' people can be really mean at times! Devotion cannot benefit us unless we use it as the guiding force to put good qualities into practice.

People often wonder how they can make the most of their time with Amma. I believe that it is by developing one of the greatest qualities a spiritual seeker can have: sincerity. Those who are able to cultivate this magical quality live lives filled with grace. Life is never easy, but sincerity allows grace to flow, guiding us around all of the obstacles that arise.

When people develop sincerity, they stop thinking only about their own little needs and desires and start focusing on helping others. Where sincerity exists, grace automatically manifests.

When we take on more service work and responsibility, stress and tension may sometimes increase, but ultimately we are rewarded with so much grace. Life is always going to be filled with hardship; there is no way to avoid this, so we might as well give something of ourselves by working hard for a good cause.

Grace reveals itself by making all of our hardships just a little bit easier to bear. As our acceptance slowly increases, our peace of mind does as well.

Not everyone is blessed with a healthy body that enables them to work as hard as they would like. But even then, when we are ready to sincerely help in some small way, we begin to grow out of selfishness (which is the whole point of spirituality).

Those with sincerity may not always be near Amma. They may not have the most beautiful singing voice, or be lucky enough to hand Amma *prasad* (a blessed offering), but they care about looking after Amma's work. Frequently they are far from Amma working in the kitchen, cleaning toilets or doing other duties that take them far away.

Amma's love flows so freely to people who work with the right attitude, to those who have expanded their heart and made a little space for others in their lives. It takes a mature outlook to forget about our own desires and take on other people's problems instead.

One of the organisers of Amma's European programs was sad when she received a slight chastisement from Amma. As the event drew to a close, Amma remarked that the program had not been arranged properly. The girl defensively replied, "Amma, other people were in charge of it!"

Amma did not relent, "Do you know how many meals were served during the program?" The girl had to admit that she did not have a clue about the dining room at all.

Amma pointed out that true sincerity should be in knowing all of the aspects of the program, especially because she was supposed to be one of the organisers. Instead of assuming that other people would do things for her, she should have looked into *all* areas of the program and made sure that they were working correctly.

Responsible, sincere action is the manifestation of true and deep devotion. This kind of devotion should serve as the building block of our relationship with Amma.

At another program, the bramachari in charge did not go to the venue ahead of time. Instead, he came late and rode with us in Amma's van. As we drove along, Amma turned to him and said, "You should have gone before us. You should have made sure everything was in order for the function. You should have looked into the meals and made sure there was enough food for everyone."

Amma's words turned out to be true. The previous day the food had run out at the program. On this morning, the people arriving were hungry and the lines for the food were enormous. Amma explained that in order to demonstrate his sincerity for Amma, this bramachari should have made sure that there was always enough food at the program.

We may think, 'I am the person in charge of this particular aspect of the program, so my duties have only to do with this or that.' But Amma ever so clearly reminds Her disciples that this is not the right way to think. Take responsibility. Check that there is enough food. Make sure *everything* is taken care of in *all* of the departments.

Sincerity certainly is one of the most valuable qualities we can have and it is not so difficult to cultivate. You do not even need to be skilled in any particular area; you only have to open up your heart and be ready to work hard. If you can express enthusiasm along with that sincerity, you will become a joy to everyone around you. They will know that you are the type of person who will always come and help whenever needed, which is such a rarity in today's selfish world.

Amma's life is the epitome of sincerity, enthusiasm and so much more, which is why seekers flock to Her from all around the world.

On a North India tour a few years back, one of the brahmacharis was sweeping the road at the end of the program. When I saw him, I thought, 'Oh, how wonderful. I would love to get a broom and do that too,' but I knew people would not let me do it for long. I was a little jealous. I kept thinking, 'What a great thing to be able to humbly sweep the street clean.'

I told one of the bramacharinis how I felt.

She admitted, "Oh, yes. I also saw him, but when I saw him, I thought, 'Ooh, let me go in the other direction. I shouldn't see this. Don't let anyone see me looking at him. Otherwise they will expect me to do it too!"

Grace comes to us according to the attitude of our mind. It is so sad that the first response of most people, when offered the opportunity to do a good deed, is, 'Oh no! Let me run as fast as I can in the other direction. If not, I may get caught having to do something I do not feel like doing – especially if Amma is not watching me do it!'

The next day while we were traveling, I had the chance to tell Amma about the bramachari who was sweeping. I was so proud to tell Her. I eagerly waited for just the right moment. "Amma," I said, "You know what this brahmachari was doing?" I wanted to put in a good word for someone and was excited to offer a little bit of praise.

Amma replied, "I know. He always does things like that." Amma knew that he was sincere. She knew she could rely on him to look into every detail of the work he did for Her. It was nothing new for him.

A few years later (in the middle of writing this book), I came across this story in my files and it re-kindled my desire to sweep. The very next day, while we were in Mangalore on a South India tour, Amma went to the stage to serve dinner to all of the devotees gathered.

I noticed that the devotees who had laid out the path for Amma (with a red carpet and lots of fancy decorations at the front of the building) had placed the path leading to a very steep set of stairs. On the other side of the building the stairs were significantly less steep.

I asked one man if he could get people to change the path. He said he would, but he was leaving it to the last minute, so I decided to change it myself. I found someone to help me, and together we moved all of the carpets and redirected the path to the shorter, less steep stairs.

Afterwards, there was sand scattered on the carpets. When all the devotees went off to have their dinner with Amma, I started sweeping it myself, as there was no one there to stop me.

I had to smile as I swept. Within 24 hours of re-reading the brahmachari sweeping story, Amma had fulfilled my desire to sweep. Amma never lets us down. She fulfils all of our desires in one way or another, when the time is right.

To make our relationship with Amma genuine and sincere, we have to channel our devotion into all of our actions – this is true spirituality. The things we tend to place into a limited category and call 'spiritual': mantra repetition, meditation, or even wearing spiritual-looking clothes and putting marks on our forehead – all fall short if we are not sincere.

How lucky we are when we receive the chance to become 'spiritual' in the truest sense of the word by doing something kind and unexpected for others. Surely, in those moments, God looks down and smiles. We underestimate the value of simple gestures of kindness. These moments may not seem so spiritual, but truly they are spirituality in its highest form.

Amma says it is our work ethic and the attitude of taking responsibility that really shows our sincerity.

It is important to always keep on trying to do good things, even if you do not feel like it – especially if you do not feel like it. Most of the time we are accustomed to following our desires, which results in constantly taking from others. Instead, we should learn to give and try to become more like Amma.

We should strive to cultivate new, positive habits while we can, before it is too late. Life is changing so quickly and it takes a long time to change ourselves. Developing good habits is difficult and takes a long time, but it is well worth the effort.

Good habits give us the strength to journey on towards understanding our true nature and why we are here on this earth. It is not to just live and die as limited individuals.

If we have sincerity in our life and faith in Amma as our guide, all of the gaps where we are lacking will be filled by Divine grace.

One devotee used to pray every day that she might walk alone on the beach with Amma. She used to pace back and forth on the beach as she recited her *archana* (prayers), all the while visualising holding hands with Amma.

Then one night, while she was walking along the beach with another girl, Amma came to the beach…*alone.* The other girl ran back to the ashram to tell everyone that Amma was out, and this girl got to walk along the beach for a long time with Amma, holding hands and talking.

Amma is a flow of love, always giving us more than we can even dream of. Ultimately, we need the Guru's grace to reach the goal, as we are not going to be able to do it by any amount of concentration that we have on our own. This is the reason why we need to develop honest sincerity and true devotion towards our Guru.

The journey to becoming genuinely compassionate and selfless is slow – but Amma's presence is a very profound blessing, reminding us of who we can become.

Chapter 12

The Divine Remedy

"Only a life lived in service is worth living."

—Albert Einstein

Selfless service is the easiest, most enjoyable spiritual practice. It is the most efficient way to purify the ever-fluctuating thoughts in our restless, agitated minds.

It is not too difficult to tune into the Divine will. It is just a matter of being practical and seeing clearly what needs to be done. Then we can move forward and try to do what is needed with a selfless attitude. We might fail on our own, but in league with Amma, miracles happen.

For days I had noticed how dirty all of the chairs in front of the *kalari* (temple) were. There were about 50 chairs, and I did not want to trouble anyone else to clean them. I had the desire to clean them all by myself.

I spoke to the *pujari* (priest) at the kalari and told him that we had to do something to get them looking better. He suggested that we buy new ones, but I knew we should be able to clean them.

I planned my strategy. I searched online and investigated the best way to clean plastic chairs. Several videos popped up, each showing a different method of chair cleaning.

The first video suggested high intensity water sprays, but I knew we could not waste the amount of water that this method would take. Spray-painting them again was the second option, but the best method suggested using lots of bleach, scrubbing them hard and then rinsing them. I realised this was my only option (but with a lot less bleach, as it is not good for the environment).

I finally got down to it. I found a scrubby and carried a bottle of bleach outside to the pile of chairs. I started on one chair. I scrubbed it delicately for a minute (people were walking past and looking at me, and I did not want them to feel that they had to help), but none of the stains seemed to disappear. I took it into my office so I could work on it properly, without being watched.

My goal was to clean all of the 40 or 50 chairs entirely by myself. But after some time, I reluctantly gave up. Despite my best efforts, the first chair was not coming clean. Dejected, I returned my chair to the pile of dirty ones, feeling like a failure. But the very next day, Amma answered my prayers by arranging a giant chair-cleaning party.

One ashram resident tells the story best:

> During *Onam* (a favourite Kerala festival) and throughout the August and September holidays, lots of extra visitors come to the ashram to celebrate with Amma. Every year, the ashram brings thousands of chairs out of storage for the festivals. Handling, organising and cleaning the chairs is part of my seva.
>
> One evening I noticed that the stacks of new chairs were much cleaner than our dirty, old ones. There was another man doing seva with me at the time, and we decided to pull out all of the old and dirty chairs and place them in the

back of the hall. We then pulled out all of the nice-looking chairs and replaced them so that all the chairs in the dining hall looked good.

Afterwards, I went to my room and started to read through some of my notes from Amma's previous satsangs. A few months earlier, Amma told us this story:

Once there was a Master, who asked his disciples to go and get one particular type of fruit from a very specific garden. When the disciples arrived at the garden they saw a giant boulder blocking the entrance. They gave up and went back to the Master to tell him it was an impossible task.

The Master noticed that one of the disciples was missing. He asked the others where the boy was. None of them knew, so the Master decided to go out and search.

The Master found his disciple at the entrance to the garden, trying with all his might to push the boulder. He asked the disciple, "What are you doing?"

The boy replied, "I'm pushing the boulder, so I can get inside and get the fruit."

The Master said, "Do you really think you can?"

The disciple replied, "Master, I know it is impossible, but my duty is to try because you said to. Only your grace can make it happen."

The Master was so touched by this attitude of surrender that he put his hand on the boulder and it split open.

Inside, the stone was full of gems and diamonds.

The morning after we had replaced all of the dirtiest chairs, Amma walked through the hall to lead the ashramites in meditation and to serve everyone a prasad lunch. Suddenly, She stopped in Her tracks and pointed to the chairs. She was talking to the people around Her and making a big deal about them. After a moment's pause, She went to lead the meditation.

Later that afternoon, while Amma was giving darshan, She called a devotee over and told him that all the chairs needed to be cleaned. She told him to take a particularly dirty chair – it was pink with all sorts of grey stains – and clean it. The stains looked like a permanent chemical discoloration that had been there for years: it was a hopelessly dirty chair.

He took the chair and, with another devotee, cleaned it in front of Amma's house. They cleaned it until it was shining like new.

Unaware of this, I came down to the dining hall a little while later to set up the chairs for bhajans and dinner as usual. After Amma serves lunch the chairs are always in complete disarray. It is my job to reset them neatly.

The serving supervisor told me that Amma said we had to clean every chair like new. She pointed out the dark grey discoloration I was expected to clean away.

I replied, "No, that's totally impossible. That spot is a chemical weathering. It can't be removed."

The supervisor disagreed saying, "It was done this afternoon. Go look!" So I took a walk over to Amma's house and saw a bright pink chair sparkling in the sunset.

I got a metal scrub brush and sighed: I guess the grey stains could be removed. I hadn't known that, even though I had been in charge of cleaning the chairs for two years.

A small part of my mind started freaking out. The thought, 'Amma must hate me. How can She possibly expect me to clean every single chair?' crept through my brain. I took a deep breath and pushed the voice aside.

I told myself, 'I am here to serve the world. I must try to do what Amma says.' I resolved to try and clean one chair.

I kept comparing my chair with the bright pink one that had been cleaned already: the legs, the outside and the inside. I had to check three times just to make sure I had cleaned every single possible part of my chair.

A few people saw me and asked me what in the world I was doing. One girl in particular was very curious when she saw me cleaning. I explained to her that Amma had asked that all the chairs be cleaned to look like new.

The girl looked around in amazement, "Every chair?" she asked. "There are thousands of them. Is it your responsibility?"

I told her that because I was in charge of the dining hall, I did feel that a good deal of the responsibility fell on me. But I also told her that I didn't think it was possible to do the job all by myself. I thought that the only way it could possibly get done was for everyone in the ashram to clean one chair. In the meantime, I figured I would do what I could.

That night Amma came for bhajans. After the first or second song, She talked at great length about the chairs. Amma told everyone that She was tired of looking at all of these dirty chairs.

Normally Amma sees the good in everything, but She is also the gardener, and the gardener sees the dirt. She said, "Get pink soap oil[1] and coconut husk. Everyone in the ashram is to clean one chair!" She must have prepared, because all of the supplies were set up in the back of the hall.

I asked if I could put up a Power-Point on the screen so that everyone who didn't speak *Malayalam* (Amma's mother tongue) would also know what to do.

After bhajans I noticed a big crowd gathered around the cleaning supplies. I thought, 'Wow, everyone is already doing it! They are skipping dinner to get started cleaning the chairs.'

---

[1] The pink soap oil in Amritapuri is manufactured at Amma's Ettimadai Univeristy campus in Coimbatore. It was designed by a chemist in Mumbai to be milder for the environment than commercial-grade soaps in India.

I went over to check it out. Who do I find, but Amma Herself, handing out one chair at a time to each ashram resident. She had distributed lunch earlier in the day, and now She was distributing chairs to everyone. The truth is, everyone was only enthusiastic to clean at first because Amma was there with us.

Somehow I found myself right next to Amma as She was passing out the chairs. I got to be with Her for some time, watching Her do seva. It was the most bizarre thing that has ever happened in my life...I had stacked and un-stacked these chairs for the last two years.

It felt like Amma was showing up in my room and cleaning it.

It was incredible to watch Her. It was like She was in an altered state. She distributed the chairs quickly and efficiently, picking up each one with only Her finger. She yelled at anyone who was standing around just watching Her and not cleaning. She passed out the dirty chairs and the clean chairs – every single chair. Each chair needed to be cleaned like new.

I felt like this was very symbolic of the spiritual path and Amma's ashram. Whether we are spiritually fit, or full of hopeless negative tendencies, Amma is going to clean us *all* like new.

Then Amma started cleaning the chairs Herself. She found one that was hopelessly dirty and starting scrubbing it with a coconut husk. After a few minutes She switched to a metal scrub brush in order to remove some of the deeper discoloration, (the discoloration I had been certain could not be removed). She showed those of us nearby how to do this as well. Like this, She was able to remove those deep, dark stains.

Then, all of a sudden, She was done. She started playing with the children nearby and looked just like a relaxed little girl. Eventually She went back to Her room and made chai for everyone. The brahmacharis passed it out with banana chips.

It was the most astonishing thing that's ever happened to me. It felt like all of the angels and devas had descended from heaven just to join us in our seva. We were all singing and dancing as we cleaned.

People were playing instruments, working together and supporting each other in the most beautiful way. Some had the hose and were rinsing all the chairs; others were passing out more materials. The rest were scrubbing away. It was so joyful. It was like a giant chair-cleaning party.

I felt like I was living in an *Awaken Children* story – or maybe a Disney movie.

One young girl scratched her hand with the scrubber, but still she refused to go home. Another small girl was protesting to her mother, "I don't want to sleep!"

There was so much energy – many of us stayed up until after three am, cleaning every single chair we could find from every corner of the ashram. It was definitely the most fun I've had in the ashram ever.

We didn't get every chair, and there is still more work to be done, but a year-long impossible job was accomplished in a single night due to the grace of a Perfect Master.

To clean the different types of stains we needed several different tools and techniques. Likewise, the spiritual Master gives us different tools to clean the dirt of our own mind: bhajans, seva, meditation and japa. Some of these techniques need to be done daily, but once in a while on special occasions, Amma uses the 'metal scrub brush' to really brush our minds clean.

In this case, She used chairs.

I was completely amazed that Amma fulfilled my desire to clean the chairs in the most practical way, with everyone working together. Even though I had made the effort to find the best cleaning method possible, the Internet never mentioned the super-cleaning power of pink soap oil and coconut husk (which was much stronger than bleach and less harmful to the environment).

On our own, we cannot accomplish so much, but when we work together with Amma, miracles definitely do happen.

When we are helping others and forgetting ourselves without expecting anything in return, we become a perfect instrument to receive Divine grace.

Chapter 13

Unfolding Lotus

*"If we cannot think solely of others for one day,
then do it for half a day.
If we cannot think solely of others for half a day,
then do it for two hours.
If not for two hours,
then one hour.
If not for one hour,
then one minute."*

—*Taitetsu Unno*

Questions are always posed to Amma regarding grace. We know that we desperately need it to make our lives successful and sweet. But the question always remains: how exactly can we receive grace?

Amma responds that only when we keep the doors of our heart open, will grace come flowing in. What is the use of sitting in a closed room and complaining that there is no sunlight or air? We must open the windows to enjoy the light and air. But how do we open the window of our heart?

Amma's answer is clear, "Effort is very important to open the heart. When you travel anywhere with Amma it is a pilgrimage and not a pleasure trip" (although pilgrimages with Amma are also the greatest of pleasures).

Amma tells the following story to explain how effort works: "A teacher wanted to help a student who habitually fell asleep in class, so he asked the student to lift an eight kg stone each time he felt sleepy in class. In due course the student lost his sleepiness. He became alert during school time and started getting good grades."

Our journey with Amma is much the same. People around the world may think that those of us traveling with Amma have such an easy time and are always living in the lap of luxury – this is often far from the truth and even laughable. The opposite is often the case; we frequently face unexpected challenges and need to troubleshoot difficult situations.

Simply walking with Amma through the crowds can be fraught with danger. We always need to be on high alert. Amma is often escorted by the police or exuberant security staff who have their orders to protect Amma, but I am invisible to them, or even worse, perceived as a threat lurking too close to Her. The police often stretch out their hands to bar me from being near Amma, and I reluctantly have to fight my way through them to fulfil my duty and remain nearby.

Crowds of people thrust out their hands to try and touch Amma and may inadvertently end up scratching me on the face or bruising my arms and that is only on the five minute walk to the stage. But I grow stronger and a little bit wiser by learning how to manoeuvre through the crowds.

It is certainly not easy being with Amma, but it is absolutely the greatest blessing in the world.

Through the years, I have often heard Amma encourage students to study hard. We pray for grace, but we have to do our bit as well by studying to the very best of our ability. We cannot get by on the wings of grace alone.

Grace only comes through effort. When Amma speaks of the flow of grace in life, She always links it together with effort. They go hand in hand: effort first, *then* grace.

When we work hard, we benefit in so many different ways. Even when we do not receive everything we hope and dream for from our efforts, we may notice that our health improves from the exercise we receive while working, and our mind will certainly expand. Seva allows us to dig more deeply into ourselves and unlock hidden potential.

Without making an effort, we will always remain average and mediocre. We are all guilty of this. No one really tries their hardest…no one but Amma.

Amma inspires us to reach so much higher than we would have ever thought possible. We are content to remain earthbound, but She gently, and oh-so-sweetly, kindles a fire beneath us, and nurtures that flame until we stretch up towards the stars, towards infinity…towards Divinity.

When the devastating earthquakes hit Nepal in 2015, I received an email from a devotee who was visiting there to go hiking. When I saw where the email was from, I was a little alarmed, thinking that he was in trouble and in need of help.

Instead, he said that he wanted to help the people affected by the disaster. He mentioned that there were a few more Amma devotees there as well, and they all wanted to reach out and help as much as they could.

Instead of trying to flee the dangerous area and save themselves, the devotees wanted to risk their own lives to assist others in need. They felt it was Amma's training that enabled them to find the courage and practical skills necessary to serve in the midst of disaster.

Their actions are just one example of the beauty that Amma is able to awaken and bring out in us – the desire to reach out of our own little selves and consider the needs of others, instead of just thinking of our own personal problems all the time.

We must have done something good in the past to have the grace to be with Amma – but we must not try to live on our spiritual savings alone. We have to continue to do good things while we can; otherwise, our grace may run out. Keep on putting positive deposits in the bank account of good karma.

If you work hard with the right attitude, forgetting yourself and striving to do the right thing at the right time, then grace will surely find you. You will find the success you desire and ultimately reach your goal...but it does require a lot of hard work.

Here is a story that illustrates this point:

My son was born with the highest level of retardation. My whole life is devoted to him. I always cook *satvik* (pure) food for him and keep him on a very specialised diet, as recommended by his doctors. We practice his exercises daily, and I am slowly teaching him the archana.

Everyday I need to take so much care. He has seizures and loses consciousness, and I often have to carry him to the hospital, sometimes in the middle of the night. If he stops breathing, I have to give him assisted breathing.

He has changed remarkably in the last 10 years. When he was a baby, he couldn't move or think at all; he was very aggressive, always kicking, biting and rejecting everything. It has taken a lot of effort, but he is now a calm, sweet and loving child.

When I came to visit Amma in the ashram for the first time, my biggest desire was to live with Her. I asked Amma if we could move to Amritapuri. She immediately agreed.

When the office informed me that all residents should aim to do eight hours of seva per day I told them, "Don't worry, I do 24."

When my visa expired, I went back to my country, as I knew I needed to get a long-term resident visa. The trouble was, in my country there is a political issue, and it is impossible to get a long-term visa for India. I decided to try anyway.

The papers I gave to the embassy were all correct and complete, but the photo of my son was not good enough for the officials. I was told that I needed to take a new one.

The photo was fine. It was clear enough, but they didn't like that his mouth was open. "He can't close his mouth," I protested. "He is a special needs child...I can hold it closed, but it won't stay closed by itself."

While I was struggling to figure out what to do, my son got very sick. I rushed him to the hospital and he was immediately placed in the ICU. So many obstacles have been there along my way – and now my son was in the ICU again, and there was no way to get a visa back to India. I tried not to feel hopeless.

I woke up at three am to drive home each day so that I could cook for him because the hospital could not accommodate his diet. During the remainder of the time, I would sit by his bedside and sing the archana to him. Night and day, I was unceasingly serving my son.

Whenever doubts or anxiety came into my mind, I would focus on the Divine names, and the fears would go away. I could hear Amma's laugh in my mind – it would scatter all the demons – and I would laugh along with Her.

I focused on seeing every person as an embodiment of the Divine. Instead of getting angry, I tried to mentally perform worship to everybody: to the hospital, the man who wouldn't give us a visa and every obstacle.

While sitting those long hours in the hospital room, I often contemplated on Amma, praying, 'Please Amma, please let me worship everyone as I know You do.'

Then, without doing anything else, all the obstacles were removed.

My son improved overnight. It was completely unexpected and felt like a pure miracle. He improved so much that the doctors allowed us a one-hour exit from the hospital. I took him straight to the photographer to get a new photo taken.

When I handed the new photograph to the Indian embassy, despite the fact that my son's mouth was still hanging open, the photograph was approved.

The embassy went through all of my paperwork again and found one paper that wasn't signed. But there was nothing I could do; my government refused to sign it.

One lady from the government was extra compassionate. She didn't know me, but she was upset on my behalf. She exclaimed, "The Indian embassy is blocking your way; it is completely crazy!"

She picked up the phone and called the embassy. She was my advocate. She told them, "You are asking for something that is illegal in our country. You know I cannot sign that paperwork."

They replied, "We need this document or no visa."

She snapped, "But it's impossible. You are blocking your clients! Can't you just give the approval?" They hung up on her.

When my son was completely better, I went to the embassy again, this time taking him with me. The man who had been so adamant about blocking our way to India took one look at him and issued our request. We received our long-term visa.

I felt as if Amma was laughing joyfully at the situation. I know that I didn't do anything much to earn Her grace. She gives grace so easily.

Sometimes people feel that God's grace will rain down and remove all obstacles if they simply pray, but I want to remind them of Amma's words, "God's grace is the good deeds that you have performed. It is nothing else." The grace comes because we have done something good.

Frankly, we have very little choice in our life. It is a little bit disappointing, isn't it? Most people hate to hear that we have so little free will.

The only choice we really do have is whether or not to do something good now. If we choose to do good, it will manifest as grace in the future.

We like to think that we are the masters of our own destiny, but in fact, all of the things we have done in the past must bear their karmic results one day. We have to accept the results from our past right here and now. Kicking and screaming is not going to scare our karmic destiny away, no matter what we believe.

Newton's third law of motion states that every action has an equal and opposite reaction, which holds just as true in spirituality as it does in physics.

When we can convince ourselves to choose a positive path over a negative one, it really will slowly erase the bad habits we have developed in the past and cut down on some of the negative karma that would have been due to come to us.

Let us strive to develop constructive habits. Everything we do now, all of the patterns we are developing, are shaping our future. We can make our future bright by doing something wonderful in this moment. That much choice we do have.

Let us try to do something incredibly simple, but magnificently beautiful – for someone else.

Chapter 14

An Impossible Miracle

"Calamities can bring growth and
Enlightenment," said the Master.
And he explained it thus:
"Each day a bird would shelter in the
withered branches of a tree that stood
in the middle of a vast deserted plain.
One day a whirlwind uprooted the tree,
forcing the poor bird to fly
a hundred miles in search of shelter-
till it finally came to a forest
of fruit-laden trees."
And he concluded:
"If the withered tree had survived,
nothing would have induced the bird
to give up its security and fly."

—A Meditation by Anthony de Mello, SJ

Amma says that a *Sadguru* (Perfect Master) can clear away some of the karma that is due to come to us, but will not necessarily take it *all* away. The grace of the Guru can change our destiny to some degree, but it is not Amma's way to try to eliminate all of our karma. Why should Amma go against Divine will?

Amma knows that everything in creation is working perfectly and that the cycle of karma has to be experienced. It is our learning process. Ultimately, the Divine cycle is all flowing perfectly.

Whatever actions we perform in life have to bear fruit; the results of our karma have to reach us. It is designed to help us grow. It is actually quite amazing, even when we perform negative actions – which have to come back to us – the Divine always sends them back in the way that will inspire the most growth within us.

Often it is the hardship and suffering we try so hard to avoid that actually leads us to spirituality and ultimately, to a deeper sense of peace.

A devotee tells an inspiring story that touches on this point:

When I was born, the doctors told my mother not to hold out any hope. I had a tumour in my brain.

My mother knew there was something wrong right from the early stages of her pregnancy. She was extremely sick and bedridden for months, but nobody could tell her why.

In the hours after my birth, my parents searched out doctor after doctor, looking for one who might lend some hope. Finally, they found someone who agreed to perform the surgery – I was barely three days old.

I was flown to a specialty hospital nearby. I almost died several times during the procedure. My heart stopped beating. It was an impossible miracle, but somehow I survived.

During childhood I was often weak and sickly, but it wasn't until I was eight that I experienced my first Grand mal seizure. I could feel myself leaving my body, and then all of a sudden, 'I' was absent. I lost consciousness for hours. A few months later it happened again.

The doctor explained that when I was a baby, it was likely that parts of my brain had been scarred during the surgery. He believed this was the cause of my seizures now.

I was put on intensive medication, which made me slow and forgetful. I often had to skip school because I was too weak to participate. The worst part though was the fear. Although only a child, I had already experienced something very close to death. I knew it could happen again, unexpectedly, at any moment.

A deep quest arose in my soul: I wanted to know where 'I' had gone during my loss of consciousness. I knew I wasn't in my body anymore, but I couldn't figure out where I had *gone*.

My parents sent me to a psychologist, thinking it might alleviate some of my anxiety. She suggested that I learn how to meditate.

I was raised in a family that was never particularly interested in spirituality, but when I started having seizures, I was compelled toward a path of spiritual practice.

In the beginning it wasn't love that propelled me forward, it was fear and an overwhelming desire to understand. Suffering brought me to the spiritual path. From this pain grew a true longing for God.

I was 14 when I first began yearning for a spiritual teacher. I liked the meditations I had been doing, but I knew I needed someone who I could learn from directly. Amma had an ashram near my parent's home, and although we had never been there, I asked my father to take me for a visit. Amma was in India at the time, so we purchased Her biography to learn more about Her.

I fell in love.

I read the biography over and over again. While my friends went out drinking, I stayed home reading, chanting and meditating.

Sometimes my best friend would call me saying, "Please come with us. You don't have to drink...I wish you would just come with us. The parties aren't any fun without you."

But our paths diverged, and I would hang up the phone and go back to my *sadhana* (spiritual practices).

When my parents wanted to give me a gift for my 18th birthday, I asked for a one-way plane ticket to India (they bought me a round-trip). The day I arrived in Amritapuri was the 18th anniversary of the surgery that saved my life. It was then that I realised Amma's subtle presence has been with me from the beginning.

When I returned home to Europe, after spending three months in Amritapuri, my life changed. I immediately moved into my local ashram. I was still too sick at that point to hold a steady job, but I could do seva…I dedicated my whole self to that.

After I met Amma, I figured I should be able to do everything She recommends a healthy person do in their spiritual practice. I fasted once a week, slept only five hours per night and worked my body to the maximum.

I was still experiencing many small seizures, along with constant, intense stomach pain from the medication that was keeping me alive.

I started getting sicker and sicker. When Amma came to visit my city, I spoke to Her about it. She was concerned. "Fasting?!" She demanded. "You're on medication – you cannot fast! You have to eat three meals a day, and you have to eat them always at the correct time."

This was the first in a series of deeply profound lessons.

I didn't want to be a burden on anyone. I only wanted to do my seva like everybody else. The trouble was, when I tried to do lots of seva my body would break down. I would start vomiting incessantly or get so sick that I couldn't get out of bed for weeks at a time.

I experienced another Grand mal seizure. I understand now what it means when people say they 'saw their life flash before their eyes.' As I lost consciousness, I watched my life flash and felt my 'Self' float away. For the first time during a seizure, I was completely relaxed. I felt Amma's presence so strongly and remained peaceful and content. I was able to accept the situation entirely.

I floated above my body for a moment, immersed in bliss, when I felt a strong tug pulling me back down. I had a moment of resistance, but I surrendered, accepted the tug and re-entered my body. In an instant, I was back and doubled over in pain.

Amma tells a story in satsang that always touches the very depths of my soul. She talks about the time that the bears and the monkeys were building a bridge with Rama to Lanka. The bears carried heavy rocks in their arms and were able to carry a lot. The little squirrel was so sad. He wanted to help too, but he couldn't carry much more than a pebble.

He had an idea: he dipped his body in the water, rolled in the sand, ran over to the construction and shook the sand off between the rocks. Like this, slowly, he deposited handful after handful of sand onto the bridge. In the end, it was the sand that acted like cement, holding those big boulders together.

The little things that he did were just as important as the big things done by the bears. The bridge couldn't have been built without his contribution.

The next time Amma came to visit, She called me aside, "There are so many new people here. You show them where to find food and water."

Amma's instruction was an answer to my prayer. I couldn't do the hard work I would have liked, but Amma still gave me a chance to serve Her children in a meaningful way. I could not help with the heavy compost seva or sustain the long hours of pot washing, but the people I helped were always so grateful.

It was a little thing, but I did what I could. I put on a smile and offered to help. Afterwards, so many people came up to me thanking me for showing them around on their first day. They told me what a difference it had made to them and how welcoming it felt to have someone looking after them.

It was amazing – I realised that *every* small thing *is* important. We don't have to be doing some huge task – even the smallest gesture can mean a lot. Just greeting someone, listening or sharing a kind word or a smile, can make such a huge difference.

My concept of spirituality has transformed.

Discipline has become taking care of my physical body so that I can serve. Before, I saw spirituality as fasting and *tapas* (austerities), but now I strive to see spirituality in every moment.

I don't expect Amma to take my illness away. Instead, Amma gives me something so much greater – She gives me a reason for living. She gives me strength to accept my situation and live my life to the fullest. She has taught me that it is always possible to find a way to give, and it is this giving that brings true joy.

I feel Amma's grace every day. It is in the stillness of a deep meditation, in the smile of a loving friend and in the joy of helping someone in need.

Many times what we experience as difficult situations or hard times are actually blessings in disguise, great teachers sent to help us grow on the spiritual path. Amma says that regardless of our circumstances in life, *happiness is a decision*. It is the decision, *'come what may, I will be happy.'*

My greatest hope is to transform all of my difficulties and challenges in life into stepping-stones of grace to help me grow and eventually attain the highest goal of life.

I still go in and out of the hospital sometimes, but every time I come back to Amma's presence, my suffering falls away and my heart finds peace.

We have to trust that whatever comes to us comes from God. It is always for our benefit and growth. Feel free to pray for whatever you want, but keep this truth in mind. What comes to us is *always* for the best. Oftentimes we pray for things that are not for our highest benefit. Instead, it would be better to surrender to Divine will.

Recently, the question was posed to Amma about whether or not it is beneficial to pray for all of the little things that we want, or if those small prayers detract from our reserve of grace when we pray for the big things?

Amma replied, "Grace does not work like that; it is *unlimited*." She went on to say that it is good to offer all of our desires to God, even the little ones, but we should also be careful. We have to remember that everything that happens is part of the Divine plan, and God's plan is better than our own.

A man once told me that as he was driving home late one night, he started to feel sleepy. At that very instant, the police pulled him over for going slightly over the speed limit. Many people in this situation would have been annoyed, but he told me he had never been so happy to see a police officer. It completely woke him up and probably saved him from an accident.

When good things happen, we have the opportunity to be grateful and offer our thanks to God, and when bad things happen, it is good to try and do the same. We can feel free to ask God for anything at all we think we want, but we must also strive to accept our present situation.

If we are able to gracefully accept all experiences, knowing there is an important lesson hidden within them, then we will always get through life's problems with joy and gratitude. Trying situations only come to make us stronger. As the saying goes, 'What doesn't kill you makes you stronger!'

Chapter 15

Surrendering to Peace

"Life always gives us
exactly the teacher we need
at every moment.
This includes every mosquito,
every misfortune,
every red light,
every traffic jam,
every obnoxious supervisor (or employee),
every illness, every loss,
every moment of joy or depression,
every addiction,
every piece of garbage,
every breath.
Every moment is the guru."

—*Joko Beck*

Sometimes we get depressed thinking about all of the negative experiences and difficulties we have experienced in the past or may experience in the future. We often complain that everything going wrong is someone else's fault. It is helpful to remember that if we view difficult experiences from an optimistic perspective, we may ultimately realise they are blessings in disguise.

We need to search for the goodness hiding in every situation. Positive thinking truly does have the power to change our destiny. Perhaps seeing the bright side of life isn't as difficult as we think.

Perhaps, as the following verses suggest, it is just child's play:

> When I look at a patch of dandelions, I see a bunch of weeds that are going to take over my yard. My kids see flowers for Mom and blowing white fluff you can wish on.
>
> When I look at an old drunk and he smiles at me, I see a smelly, dirty person who probably wants money and I look away. My kids see someone smiling at them and they smile back.
>
> When I hear music I love, I know I can't carry a tune and don't have much

rhythm, so I sit self-consciously and listen. My kids feel the beat and move to it. They sing out the words. If they don't know them, they make up their own.

When I feel wind on my face, I brace myself against it. I feel it messing up my hair and pulling me back when I walk. My kids close their eyes, spread their arms and fly with it, until they fall to the ground laughing.

When I pray, I say thee and thou and grant me this, give me that. My kids say, "Hi God! Thanks for my toys and my friends. Please keep the bad dreams away tonight. Sorry, I don't want to go to Heaven yet. I would miss my Mommy and Daddy."

When I see a mud puddle, I step around it. I see muddy shoes and dirty carpets. My kids sit in it. They see dams to build, rivers to cross and worms to play with.

I wonder if we are given kids to teach or to learn from? No wonder God loves the little children! Enjoy the little things in life, for one day you may look back and realise they were the big things.

—*Author Unknown*

If it is not pleasant where we are, then it is up to us to put in efforts to redecorate or move on…but the truth is, far more often than not, the outside world refuses our efforts to change it. What can we do? Our only choice is to try and adjust our mindset.

When we fight against our circumstances, take things for granted or are quick to blame and judge, life will become extremely uncomfortable for us. Everything comes to us *exactly* as we need. This may be a painful truth to swallow, but it really is the best understanding to live by.

The whole world and everything in creation is unfolding the way it should, so why wish for things to be different? Everything that comes to us, even the most painful experiences, come only to teach us the important lessons we need to learn.

Anthony J. D'Mello tells a beautiful story illustrating this point:

There was once a rabbi who was revered by the people as a man of God. Not a day went by when a crowd of people wasn't standing at his door seeking advice, healing or the holy man's blessing.

There was, however, in the audience a disagreeable fellow who never missed a chance to contradict the master. He would observe the rabbi's weaknesses and make fun of his defects, to the dismay of the disciples, who began to look on him as the devil incarnate.

One day the 'devil' took ill and died. Everyone heaved a sigh of relief. Outwardly, they looked appropriately solemn, but in their hearts they were glad. But to most people it was a big surprise to see their master plunged into genuine grief at the funeral.

When asked by a disciple later if he was mourning over the eternal fate of the dead man, he said, "No, no. Why should I mourn over our friend, who is now in heaven? It was for myself I was grieving. That man was the only friend

I had. Here I am, surrounded by people who revere me. He was the only one who challenged me. I fear that with him gone, I shall stop growing."

As he said those words, the master burst into tears.

Two people may be experiencing the same type of pain, but if one looks at it with a mind filled with discrimination and acceptance, then that person will soon find peace. If the other person simply complains all the time, then he or she will endlessly suffer. It is our attitude and the way we look at situations that infuses us with the necessary strength to accept them.

Amma is a Divine catalyst for our karma to either fructify or diminish. It happens automatically, both in Her presence and far away, for those who can focus their attention on Her. Praying to Amma has caused so many miracles to happen all around the world.

In conversations with devotees, one hears story after story of the incredible grace that has manifested in their lives and the lives of those they know. But that does not mean all of our external problems and ailments will automatically disappear.

Amma will not remove all of our obstacles. Instead, when it all seems too much for us, She often lessens our pain and suffering and gives us the strength to deal with everything we have to go through. That is the beauty and wisdom of Her Divine, motherly love for us.

A devotee sent me a letter. He was feeling sad upon his mother's passing and needed to share his feelings:

> ...Just a short note before you start traveling. I am thinking about you and praying for you as you begin to travel again. I have been off work for two months now, so unfortunately I do not have the resources to travel and see Mother right now. I am hoping that by the time you are on the East Coast, I might be able to drive up to DC and attend the programs there. It is in God's hands as always.
>
> I have really been missing Mother these past few days. Sadness for my mother's suffering, and the suffering of

so many human beings, has been with me. I'm not a big fan of sadness, but I am trying to pray and be productive with it (although I'm failing miserably most of the time).

God's ways are so far beyond my ways. Some days I am able to put one foot in front of the other and work with a full heart – but other days the sadness sets in.

My mom suffered so much during her final days. She was completely unable to let go. She spent one day growling like a wounded animal, kicking and screaming in her bed. We tried to comfort and console her, but nothing helped. After a few hours we gave up trying to calm her down. I had my brother help me put pillows all around her hospital bed in an attempt to keep her from hurting herself while she thrashed around.

I told her, "Okay, Mom, I get it. You're frustrated and you're angry. This is hard for you, and I see that – so go ahead – fight it for as long as you need to. We will try to keep you safe."

She continued to growl and thrash for some time, but eventually exhausted herself. It was a dramatic representation of what I do when I am not surrendered to the will of God.

In my soul I sometimes fight the very source of love, demanding it look like I want it to, but I realise now that saying "No!" to God is always going to bring suffering. I am trying to learn from my mother's experience.

Surrender, true surrender, is much more difficult than it sounds like it should be.

Fear drives me often, even against my will. So I try again today. Again and again I pray for the ability to surrender to Her, to Her love, Her guidance and Her will.

Often I thrash around in my refusal to accept the Divine will. I pray for the eyes of my soul to be opened, to be able to walk along this path with faith and gratitude instead of fear.

I am selfish, childish and lazy so often – and yet Amma is so patient with me and takes me back every time. I pray I can learn to surrender so that in the end I can pass with less suffering than I just witnessed in my mother's passing…

Life is never easy, especially when times are hard, but we should never give up hope. Despair will only lead to painful suffering. If we pray with sincerity for the needed strength, we will find it and be able to cope with anything that comes. With grace, we can endure what we have to. Nothing is ever given to us that is too much for us to handle. God knows what is best for us, even though this may seem hard to believe at times.

One of the men who came to Amma for darshan asked Her, "Why did God give us this human birth?"

Amma's answer to him was, "Son, don't trouble yourself to think about this now. It has already happened; you have already taken birth. Just try to find a way that you can use this birth to help people."

Surrender and acceptance in hard times is extremely difficult, but as one comes to love Amma, everything becomes a little sweeter and so much easier.

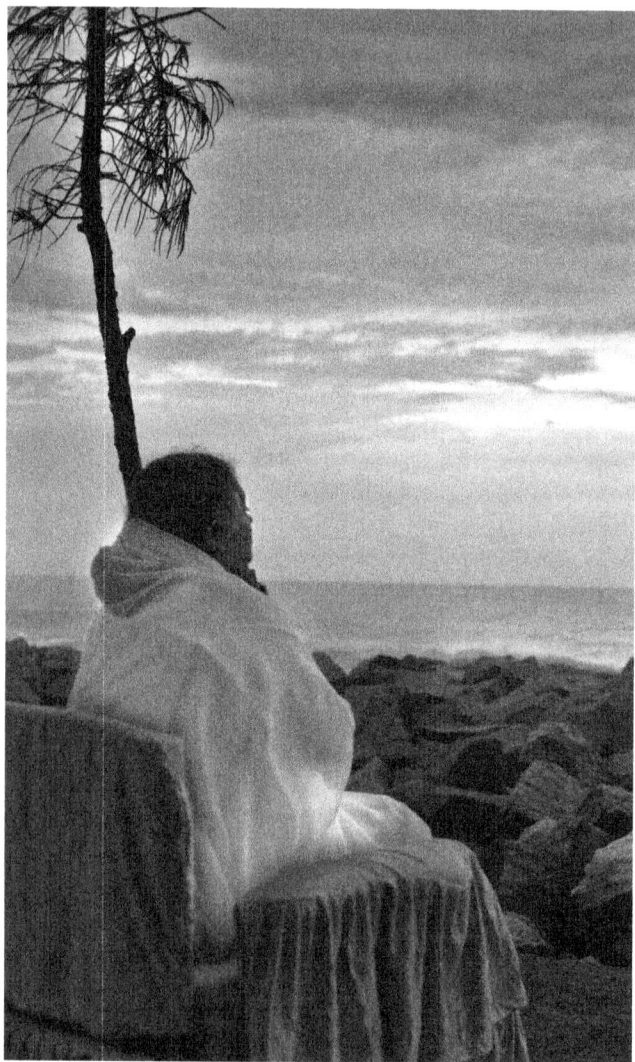

Chapter 16

The Pain of The World

"Love and compassion are necessities,
not luxuries.
Without them, humanity cannot survive."

—*The Dalai Lama*

During the times we are faced with painful karma that cannot be changed or lessened, we need to turn towards faith and prayer. God's grace can flow to us in the form of strength, surrender and acceptance.

We are often reminded that our inherent nature is all-powerful, as Divinity lies dormant inside us all. We are created in the image of God. If we endeavour to turn inside and tap into our full potential, we will find that we can bear whatever karma we have to. When challenges arise, we need to work out how to tap into this inner storehouse of power.

Sometimes it seems impossible to find the goodness in situations. Unfortunately, that is just the way karma reveals itself from time to time. If Amma does not take away the pain during such times, She will help us to find the strength to bear whatever we have to, if we let Her.

Here is another story from Amma's orphanage demonstrating the power of the human soul to bear any sorrow:

My name is Lakshmi. Sri Mata Amritanandamayi Devi is my mother; 'mother' means the one who made me what I am today.

I do not know anything about my birth, my birthplace, or my house. I do not even know the name of my father. My biological mother was called Leena. The story she told me was this:

My parents were in love. After marriage, father started showing his true colours. He began drinking, and soon it was a daily occurrence for him to come home drunk and abuse my mother. When I was around three and a half, I was put in a nursery. One day my father came there drunk and beat up my teacher. After that, I didn't go to school.

I had three siblings: two brothers and one younger sister. The boys left home early due to poverty and abuse. My mother, my sister and I were only able to survive by begging. When we couldn't go out to beg or when we received no alms, we went hungry. We lived in tattered clothes.

We had a small hut to lie down in and sleep. One day when father came home drunk, he set fire to the house. After that, we started sleeping on the verandas of shops. Unable to carry the burden of extreme poverty, mother took my sister into the sea and drowned her. When she came to grab me, I ran away.

We started begging on trains. While we were somewhere in Tamil Nadu, as a train was approaching, my mother grabbed me and tried to put our heads down on the track. Out of intense fear, I managed to wriggle away, but my mother died there.

After that, someone took me by the hand and brought me to his house. I was not even five then. He was in need of a servant, but soon he realised that my undernourished body was too frail to serve him. After that, he no longer gave me food. He started beating me. He decided to return me to the same place where he found me.

A neighbour came to know about this and brought me to Amma's orphanage in Parippally. That is how the relationship between Amma and me started.

When the Onam holidays came around, I saw everyone preparing to go home (many children had a home, but their parents were not able to look after them, so they lived in Parippally).

I became sad: I had no home, no mother, no one. Then, a swami told me that he would take me to a mother who is full of love. The swami's words were true. When I had my darshan for the first time, my love towards Amma was bountiful.

When Amma came to know that I could not read or write, She Herself started teaching me. She started with the alphabet. While darshan was going on, She would make me sit by Her side and write the Malayalam letters on a slate. Thus, I learned to write and read in Her presence. From then on, Amma always made sure I had everything I needed.

When Amma's South Indian Tour came around, I asked Her if I could go with Her. She said She would take me with Her only if I wrote what She taught me and showed it to Her. I studied hard and met Amma's condition. Thus, for the first time, I travelled with Amma to Madurai. Regardless of how busy She was, Amma used to call me to Her room.

When I was about 20, Amma asked me whether I wanted an ashram life or a married life. I replied that I wanted to get married. Without much delay, Amma found a husband for me. She performed my wedding, giving me the required gold ornaments and the bridal sari.

Today we have two sons. Due to Amma's kindness, our life is very happy. When I go to the ashram now, Amma receives us happily; welcoming us just like any mother would welcome home a married daughter.

I just can't imagine a life without Amma.

Many times we may think that we have a lot of personal problems, but it is humbling for us to understand that there are countless people in the world who are suffering tremendously (and not just feeling a little uncomfortable like we sometimes do).

With all of the suffering in the world today, we honestly do not realise how lucky we are. If we all threw our problems into a pile and were able to see everyone else's – we would quickly want to take back our own. We truly are much more fortunate than most people. Here are some sobering reminders:

- 80% of the world's population lives on less than $10 a day.

- 1.3 billion people live on less than $1.25 a day (30% of these desperately poor live in India).
- 805 million people worldwide do not have enough food to eat.
- More than 750 million people lack adequate access to clean drinking water.
- 1 billion children are living in poverty and 22,000 children die every day as a result.

We live in a desperately unequal world where the 62 richest individuals in the world possess as much wealth as *half of the world's population combined!*

If you have good health, a fridge full of food, clothes on your back, a roof over your head and a place to sleep, you are wealthier than a huge proportion of the world's population.

If you have never experienced the horror of war, the solitude of prison, the pain of torture, or the threat of death from starvation, then you are better off than millions.

Thousands come every day to receive Amma's embrace in an effort to escape the pain of their difficult lives and find a solution to their problems.

Amma shared a story that represents the kind of sorrows She hears during darshan. There was a family of four – a mother, father and two children. Both the parents worked. The mother cooked some food and then went to work. For lunch she ate the food she had cooked, but one of the vegetables she had used in the dish had become poisonous.

After she ate it, she died from food poisoning. When her husband heard the news, he immediately thought of the children, who had taken the same food with them to school. He did not have a phone, so he jumped on his motorbike and rushed to the school to try to stop his children from eating the food.

Tragically, he met with an accident on his way there, and he died as well. He was not able to stop the children from eating their lunch. They met the same fate as their mother.

This is just *one* unimaginably sad story out of the many that Amma listens to as She sits for hours and hours every day, listening to person after person relate their tragedies and their triumphs to Her.

Amma knows that compassion is the best solution for the world's problems. Of course, this does not mean that we break down and cry out of compassion for others. Instead, we ought to seek out positive and practical solutions to help solve problems. Compassion in action is the real solution we need to address the difficult situations in today's world.

This is why Amma eats a bare minimum of food every day. She takes the absolute least for Herself and strives to *give* the utmost maximum to society, for She feels the pain of all those who are suffering.

One of the ashram residents shared with me that during a period when Amma held extremely long darshan days just before leaving for a European tour, She was so exhausted that She said, "I just can't go on. I am going to collapse…I am going to collapse. Get ready to catch me."

This woman (who was doing seva next to Amma, helping the devotees to their feet after they received darshan) did not know whether she should catch the people who were coming out of Amma's arms or try to catch Amma Herself. She was feeling so bad for Amma and then, as so often happens, Amma instructed, "Call 50 more people for darshan!"

Amma always goes beyond the point of exhaustion, beyond the point where you or I might decide that we just cannot go on. She crosses this line consistently and still does more, but lovingly, not begrudgingly like we might if we tried the same thing. She knows that with an attitude of pure love...one can do absolutely *anything*.

When we arrived in Switzerland this past tour, Amma was thoroughly exhausted. She was in so much pain She could hardly move. When She got to Her room, She collapsed on Her bed (which had been made up on the floor).

A couple of hours later, while we were setting up the bookstore for the next day's program, who should come to the dining hall to serve food to everyone? Amma...

No matter how She may be feeling, there is simply no stopping Her from trying to make everyone happy. Nowhere else in the world will we find the same kind of compassionate Divine love and sacrifice that we behold in Amma. The depth of Her compassion is absolutely unimaginable.

Chapter 17

Embracing Life

> *"Surrender to grace.*
> *The ocean cares for each wave*
> *until it reaches the shore.*
> *You are given more help than*
> *you will ever know."*

—*Rumi*

It truly is amazing what we can achieve when we put in our maximum effort and tap into the enormous potential we hold inside. It is always inspiring when we see or hear about people who have gone beyond the limitations we tend to impose upon ourselves.

The following is a true story about a young man who defied all odds, armed only with the power of kindness:

In England there was a young teenage student whose father died of a brain tumour. He felt sad and lonely because of this.

He kept photos of his father in his locker at school, but some of the other kids tore these down and bullied him. For a long time he kept away from everyone.

Then one day he decided to make an effort to go beyond his pain. He decided to reach out and do something totally simple, just for the sake of kindness.

He started opening the door at school for everyone and saying, "Good morning," to each person who walked through the door. It was such an ordinary gesture, but it began to have a profound effect on people at the school. They were not used to anyone acting so considerately towards them.

He became a great role model, gradually influencing many of his classmates to be strong, courageous and go beyond their personal problems to help others. He went on to become an inspiring public speaker and leader. All this sprouted from the small seed of a selfless thought and the bravery it took to follow through on a simple, kind action.

If we are attempting to transform and really striving to change our ways for the better, our suffering will automatically lessen over time. When our focus drifts away from thinking only about our own needs and begins to focus on helping others, the world becomes a little bit brighter and, actually, not so bad after all.

It is not the really big things we do that make us great but the small things we do with a good attitude. The best example of this is Amma's embrace. She is transforming the world one hug at a time. No matter how hard things are, when we hold onto faith and reach out to do something kind, we can overcome anything.

Even with all the problems we have, coming to the holy presence of Amma makes us some of the most blessed people on this planet. We have the opportunity to witness first-hand the joy and love that Amma bestows upon the world.

Because of Amma's compassion and the devotees' sincere faith, Her touch brings about a transformation in people's lives.

A devotee tells a beautiful story about how Amma transformed her:

> Amma saved my life. Literally. I am fairly certain that I would have put an end to this precious life if it wasn't for Amma and the way She guided me to find exactly what I needed to get through one of the most difficult periods of my journey.
>
> I had been struggling with depression and severe anxiety since I was about seven and my father was killed in a car accident. From that point, most of my time was spent searching for ways to heal the little girl who seemed frozen in time.
>
> By my early 40's my life had completely fallen apart. My psychotherapy practice collapsed and along with it went my mental health. I lost my home and was living out of my car.
>
> I spent the days chanting my mantra, looking at photos of my favourite Saints and Avatars, and crying to Mother. Early mornings and late nights were occupied with carefully crafted strategies to hide

from park rangers, hunters and large animals, since my bed was now in state parks and remote forests.

When Amma came to my city, I felt that even after 11 years under Her care as my Guru, it might just be my last darshan. I didn't have a plan yet, but I no longer wanted to be in this body. I was so tired.

As I sat in the darshan line, I felt very far away from myself. When I reached Amma, I didn't look at Her. I was too ashamed. I told Her nothing about how I was feeling. I had sobbed in Her arms during my last darshan and couldn't bear another round of everyone telling me that they saw my darshan and asking what was wrong.

As She pulled me toward Her, I felt nothing. She held me for a long time and started to whisper something intently in my ear. The whisper got louder and more intense. I was startled to realise that She was speaking to me in a full English sentence. I struggled to become more present and listen.

I couldn't believe my ears, "I want to live. I Want To Live. I Want To LIVE. I WANT TO LIVE!"

As Amma continued, I thought, 'Oh my God, She knows!' and then, 'Of course, She knows!'

She gazed deeply into my eyes. In that moment, I experienced what Amma actually meant when She spoke those words, "I – the Eternal Self – wants to live in me, through me, with me."

In a split second, I felt a deep stillness, an awareness – a living presence that was untouched by the ghost of depression and anxiety masquerading as 'my' identity.

Amma motioned to the floor next to Her chair, but before She did, She handed me an apple with my prasad.

I sat down beside Amma and Her whisper became a rhythm in my mind, "I want to live. I want to live. I want to live." I began to chant these words as if they were a new mantra that She had given me. For the first time, I could identify with my True Self, the Eternal Mother, inside of me. Amma had planted a seed.

Another month passed but the mind's depression still had not lifted. Being a psychotherapist myself, I knew that psychiatric meds were a last resort and I did not want to take them, but I felt I had no choice. Even though I wasn't fully sold on the idea of living, Amma had given me such a sweet glimpse of who I really am that I decided not to take my own life.

The mind was no longer quite as convincing as it once had been, even though it raged on loudly, trying every trick to hook me into identifying with misery and judgment. But I fought it and sent a message to a friend in India at the Amritapuri ashram, asking her to ask Amma about medication. Amma sent back the message that, "Yes, I should take medicine."

I tried my first course of psych drugs. The only effects I had were side effects.

The first one I tried created heart palpitations and feelings of suffocation. The only thing that made these side effects stop was gallons of water mixed with *Atma Puja* water (holy water blessed by Amma).

The next medicine created a manic effect. Although the house and car became very, very, *very* clean...the medicine did nothing to help my state of mind.

Over and over I asked myself, 'Why would Amma tell me to take medicine if it doesn't work?' My faith was firm. I knew that if Amma said I needed to be on medication, that it was true, but I just couldn't figure out why it wasn't working. Finally the answer dawned...maybe I am taking the *wrong type* of medication.

I went to a medical doctor. My thyroid was not functioning properly. I was nutrient deficient, and my body was in the process of shutting down. It wasn't psychological. It was medical. Over the next several years, the doctor struggled to find the right dosage of thyroid medicine while I focused on the nutritional and spiritual aspects of healing.

As soon as the medication and nutritional foundations were in process, I began to increasingly identify with the Eternal Self within, the Self that Mother had showed me through Her darshan.

I slowly began to notice that my relationship to the depression, anxiety and everything else in life changed. The psychological mind and emotions became less and less convincing.

I was given a glimpse of my True Self: the one who perceives the mind and is the witness to the mind, the one who cannot be moved, the one who is unconditionally free.

Because of Mother's Grace, I am still in this body and able to tell my tale and, more importantly, I know who I AM.

Mother saved my life by showing me that I *am* Life.

For so long we have been thinking that we are the body, the mind and the emotions. We cling desperately onto every passing feeling that drifts through us, taking *that* as our reality. When we completely identify with the body and its changing emotions, it is impossible for us to believe that we are, in essence, a part of the Supreme consciousness.

But when we are guided back to our centre, we start to experience the inner peace that was there all along.

Amma has achieved the almost impossible task of freeing Her Self from the bondage of human conditioning with all of its associated desires, fears and pain. This is why She is able to embody and express the inherent Divinity and love that lies within us all. Unfortunately, we are not able to recognise this yet, so we keep the precious pearl of Divinity trapped within.

Amma will never judge us, never love some more than others or heal one person instead of another. She does not work like that. Grace carries Her blessings to those who invoke them in the right way, wherever they may be.

Our life manifests according to the attitudes we bring into play. We are the ones who have to manifest the strength inside to change ourselves.

It is entirely up to us. When we make the effort, the floodgates of grace are opened.

Chapter 18

Facing Death

"Please, don't worry so much, because in the end, none of us have very long on this earth. Life is fleeting, and if you're ever distressed, cast your eyes to the summer sky when the stars are strung across the velvety night. And when a shooting star streaks through the blackness, turning night into day…make a wish and think of me. Make your life spectacular."

—*Robin Williams, in the movie "Jack"*

We need to be stronger than ever and pull ourselves up into goodness, by living a life of righteousness however we can. This is the only way to find happiness in these unsteady times.

If we sow seeds of goodness, then good will come back to us, but if we do not, we are doomed to suffer.

We are living in the Kali Yuga. Sadly, the value system is in steady and rapid decline everywhere, but we cannot escape the fact that peace and harmony will only be found if we live with positive values.

I read a story about a Holocaust survivor who saw his whole family – his wife and all of his children – shot before his eyes. He realised in that moment that the Nazis could take everything away from him, everything except his peace of mind. He knew that he would only lose his mental strength if he gave in to feelings of hatred and fear. He decided to choose love.

Somehow, he mustered up the strength inside of himself to control his mind and transform his flow of negative thoughts into surrender and acceptance. In an act of true courage, he chose peace.

We cannot control the world around us. The only thing we can try to control is the state of our own mind. It is urgent that we make an effort and strive to do this. If we sincerely try, then Amma's grace will be drawn towards us like a magnet. It can carry us like a wave towards ultimate peace and fulfilment, no matter what our external circumstances may be.

During a question and answer session with Amma on the seaside of Amritapuri, someone asked, "Amma, can you set another goal for me? I just do not think I can ever achieve God realisation. I could never become like you in a million lifetimes. Isn't there something else I can strive for – something more realistic?"

Amma replied that God realisation, the end of all suffering, is the ultimate goal of life and *is* possible if we put in effort. We have a living Master, and if we strive to earn Her grace, however we can, Self realisation will become a reality for us.

She went on to say that we already *are* Amma; we just have to remove the unnecessary layers hiding this truth. Amma is already inside of us, closer than the closest. She is the jewel residing in the lotus of our heart.

In essence, we are pure. We fill ourselves with so many negative thoughts that it is hard to achieve much change.

Amma has mentioned that traditionally, the Guru would not give meditation to most disciples until they had been with him for many years. The Guru would look deeply into the mental capacity of each disciple and judge what spiritual practices were appropriate for his or her growth.

Real meditation is an uninterrupted flow of contemplation on God. If you honestly think about it, when you are sitting down to meditate, how many seconds do you actually have of totally uninterrupted thoughts about God? I bet most of us are lucky if we get 10 seconds in an hour, and that would be on a good day.

In the past, meditation was usually the final practice given. In fact, disciples would have to perform service for several years before they would receive any spiritual teachings at all. After long years of service, they would finally gain the purity and subtlety of mind to be ready for meditation. Then the Guru might recite a sacred mantra of just a few syllables that would send them soaring into high spiritual states.

Times have changed. The Guru can give us loads of service to perform, shout epics of spiritual mantras into our ears, and even sing and dance for us – but still we can be *so* stubborn as to stay rooted in our selfishness and remain unwilling to change.

Amma offers us the perfect balance of sadhana in the form of selfless service, meditation, mantra repetition and group prayers, all while humbly exemplifying through Her actions so many subtle, good qualities. She knows that for most of us selfless service is the easiest way to purify our wilful, arrogant egos.

Straight from the very beginning of our spiritual lives, we can experience the joy of devotion by performing selfless acts of service.

Amma often reminds us that our time on Earth is limited: "Remember children, this is only a rented body. At some point, we will be asked to leave it. Then we must depart. Before we leave, that which is eternal should be gained while residing in this body. If we have a house of our own, we can happily move out when we are asked to vacate this rented one. Then we can live in the eternal house of God."

There is a traditional story about a great devotee named Eknath. Once a man asked him, "Oh revered one, your life is so pure. It is sinless, you do not compete with anyone and you do not quarrel with anyone. How is it possible to live such a beautiful life?"

Eknath said, "Forget about my life; I have a suspicion about you. From today onwards count seven days; on the seventh day you will leave this earth."

The man was terrified. He knew the words of Eknath always came true. He rushed home. He spoke to no one. Nothing caught his attention. He finished all of his commitments and somehow made it through six days.

On the seventh day Eknath came to meet him. Upon seeing Eknath the man jumped up and prostrated.

"How are you?" Eknath asked.

"Everything is over for me," he replied.

Eknath asked him, "In the last six days how many sins did you commit? Did any sinful thought occur in your mind?"

The man replied, "Swamiji, I didn't have time to think of sin. I was always contemplating death waiting for me."

Smilingly, Eknath said, "Perhaps now you have the answer to your question of why I am able to lead a simple life."

We do not know how long we will live. Our life is given to us as a precious opportunity, and the days are marching by so quickly. Honestly, all we can do is take each day as if it were our last and try to be the nicest, most selfless human being we possibly can, while we have the chance.

A volunteer shared with me of some of his humbling experiences:

> I have brought countless numbers of terminally ill people to Amma in wheelchairs, etc., and I am always blown away by how Her grace and love comes through them.
>
> I am always amazed and completely humbled by those who are really sick coming for Amma's darshan, in spite of all of their physical and mental challenges.
>
> There are a few devotees I was blessed with the job of bringing for what was to be their last darshan.
>
> There was a woman in Iowa who had terminal cancer. She was in a wheelchair with her partner by her side. After I brought her for darshan, she told me

quietly that she knew Amma had heard her prayer: that her partner not be lonely when she passed. I was brought to tears by her love and generosity towards her partner. I know I am not capable of such love.

Another woman came from hospice this year. She insisted she be permitted to be with Amma as much as possible. Her friends came to me and we worked out an area where her chair could be plugged in, as there was machinery she needed for breathing. The woman wanted to stay up and be around Amma as much as possible.

When I brought her for her first darshan, Amma asked her very seriously what the doctor had said. She replied with the most beautiful, loving smile, in such a happy tone, "They say I'm going to die Amma...they say I'm going to die." Then she said, "I love you so much Amma; I love you so much!"

I have to go behind the back of the stage at times like these as the emotion becomes too much for me. I have to take a minute to breathe and cry.

I once brought a five-year-old boy with cancer to Amma. Just as we got close, he completely collapsed, unconscious. His sweet mother panicked a bit and said, "What do we do now? What do we do now?"

"Don't worry," I said.

I scooped him up and told his mom to go for her darshan. She went, and as Amma held her, the woman's tears fell and merged into Amma's sari. I carried the little boy to Amma and held him as She gave him what was to be his last darshan in this realm.

I could go on and on…I do not know why I have been given such grace. I am in tears myself as I think of the great privilege Amma gives me to help Her children to Her in their final moments of this life. I don't understand any of it.

Amma never forces Herself on anyone. She merely offers Herself in the same way as a pure river offers its water to those who are dying of thirst. The grace of God, in the form of the Guru, comes to cool us in the hot desert with Her gentle breeze. This grace is more powerful than any fate destined to befall us.

Amma shines a bright light, showing us the way to move forward through difficult times. The external world will always be full of troubles, but we can overcome them with sincere effort and the right attitude. There is nothing greater than the power of love shining light on our path.

Truly we have nothing to be afraid of. In the darkest of times, the memory of Amma's love will be the talisman to always protect us.

So rise. Serve Amma in other people. Rise out of the negativity that tries to engulf us. Break free from darkness and do beautiful things. Work towards earning Divine grace, however you can.

Honestly, the grace from Amma is so very easy to earn. Just take an innocent attitude and genuinely try to do what good you can, in whatever capacity you can – then Divine grace will embrace you…and carry you towards the goal.

CPSIA information can be obtained at www.ICGtesting.com
Printed in the USA
BVOW06s0357210516

448956BV00004B/5/P